Parenting Boys

An Effective Parenting Guide for Raising Teen Boys

(A Comprehensive and Supportive Reference to Help Your Child Recover From Addiction)

Robert Taylor

Published by Rob Miles

© **Robert Taylor**

All Rights Reserved

Parenting Boys: An Effective Parenting Guide for Raising Teen Boys (A Comprehensive and Supportive Reference to Help Your Child Recover From Addiction)

ISBN 9781990084324

All rights reserved. No part of this guide may be reproduced in any form without permission in writing from the publisher except in the case of brief quotations embodied in critical articles or reviews.

Legal & Disclaimer

The information contained in this book is not designed to replace or take the place of any form of medicine or professional medical advice. The information in this book has been provided for educational and entertainment purposes only.

The information contained in this book has been compiled from sources deemed reliable, and it is accurate to the best of the Author's knowledge; however, the Author cannot guarantee its accuracy and validity and cannot be held liable for any errors or omissions. Changes are periodically made to this book. You must consult your doctor or get professional medical advice before using any of the suggested remedies, techniques, or information in this book.

Upon using the information contained in this book, you agree to hold harmless the Author from and against any damages, costs, and expenses, including any legal fees potentially resulting from the application of any of the information provided by this guide. This disclaimer applies to any damages or injury caused by the use and application, whether directly or indirectly, of any advice or information presented, whether for breach of contract, tort, negligence, personal injury, criminal intent, or under any other cause of action.

You agree to accept all risks of using the information presented inside this book. You need to consult a professional medical practitioner in order to ensure you are both able and healthy enough to participate in this program.

Table of Contents

INTRODUCTION 1

CHAPTER 1: WHAT IS PARENTING? 3

CHAPTER 2: TANTRUMS 5

CHAPTER 3: SELF-ESTEEM AND THE MIDDLE YEARS 16

CHAPTER 4: THE MODERN KID 21

CHAPTER 5: AGGRESSION, TANTRUMS AND OTHER CHALLENGING BEHAVIORS 33

CHAPTER 5: PARENTING THE INNER CHILD 42

CHAPTER 7: SINGLE MOM WITH A BABY - THE UNIQUE CHALLENGE OF 0SINGLE MOTHERHOOD 50

CHAPTER 8: TRUTH ABOUT TEACHERS 62

CHAPTER 9: GUIDING CHILDREN 71

CHAPTER 10: YOUR DAUGHTER'S DEVELOPMENT: THE SCIENCE OF GROWING UP 80

CHAPTER 11: HOW TO RAISE HAPPY TEENAGERS 84

CHAPTER 12: SPONTANEITY & A BABY? IT IS POSSIBLE: ... 91

CHAPTER 13: THE ILL MANNERED TEEN 97

CHAPTER 14 105

CHAPTER 15: SMART PARENTING CAN HELP IN THE DEVELOPMENT OF THE CHILD 112

CHAPTER 16: HOW TO BUILD A STRONG RELATIONSHIP WITH YOUR CHILD 127

CHAPTER 17: COMMON DISCIPLINE MISTAKES PARENTS MAKE 134

CHAPTER 18: SINGLE DAD: REWARDS FOR GOOD BEHAVIOR KIDS WILL LOVE 150

CHAPTER 19: GROWING LIKE A WEED 157

CHAPTER 20: BE A TREND-SETTER TO YOUR STEP CHILDREN 171

CHAPTER 21: WHAT DO I DO IF I FIND MY TEENAGER IS USING TECHNOLOGY IN AN INAPPROPRIATE WAY? 176

CHAPTER 22: LESSON ON PARENTAL AUTHORITY 179

CONCLUSION 184

Introduction

This book contains proven steps and strategies on how to establish a successful parenting that brings fruitful impacts simultaneously on your children and you as parents.

Positive parenting is one of the fundamentals in marriage, provided that constructing a family is considered one of the essentials aims of vast majority of married people. Children have the right to enjoy being healthily, lovingly and absolutely properly parented and taken care of, so as for them to grow into productive and mentally healthy individuals who would have a prosperous and bright future, thanks to their parents' effort, awareness, discipline and responsibility. The topic of parenting has been intensively investigated, with a plenty of researches and studies having so far been conducted about it. This book, in turn, would hopefully be an effective aid to facilitate and clarify to you, reader, what parenting revolves around and what factors are required for its success.

Thanks again for downloading this book, I hope you enjoy it!

Chapter 1: What Is Parenting?

Fundamentally, parenting is the raising of a child or children from infancy to adulthood by the biological parents. However, aside from the biological parents of a child or children, mostly in developing countries, relatives such as; an older sibling, a grand-parent, an aunt, uncle or any other family member or a family friend could assist in parenting a child. As parents, you do not play favorites and must always try to be consistent as possible in handling the children.

According to "Wikipedia," parenting also known as, "Child rearing," is the process of promoting and supporting the physical, emotional, social, spiritual and intellectual development of a child or children from infancy to adulthood. The most essential fundamental bonding between parents and their children starts with the parenting style or technique applied by parents in caring for their kids.

Naturally, the most common and realistic partakers in parenting a child from infancy to adulthood are the biological parents, (Father and Mother). However, circumstances can introduce a change in this common practice of parenting, thereby opening the door to other persons, ranging from the elder sibling to grand-parents, even to aunts or uncles. In some cases, people from outside the family block might be involved in parenting the children, whether the biological parents are near home or far from home.

Chapter 2: Tantrums

We've all been there, out in public, proud of our little toddler behaving like such an angel, thinking we are the best parent in the world. Within seconds, all has fallen apart, the toddler has destroyed something, everyone is looking at us as the toddler screams, tears rolling down their cheeks, and suddenly we feel like crawling under a rock. Our world is shaken, and we feel as if we are the worst parent in the world.

As it turns out, we are not bad parents. Believe it or not, it is hardwired into your child to behave this way as much as we do not enjoy it. Scientists now know that between that ages of 18 months and 4 years, toddlers have almost no control over this type of behavior. This is great news for parents who have been beating themselves up for years, trying to figure out what they are doing wrong and why their little angel turns into a spawn from the dark regions of the Earth when it is least expected.

The good news is that these tantrums are not your fault as the parent and these tantrums do not mean that your toddler is a bad child. What it does mean is that these outbursts come as naturally to your toddler when he or she is filled with emotion as yawning comes to you when you are tired.

For those that do not know a lot about the different areas of the brain and how they function, there is an area just behind your forehead that is called the prefrontal cortex. This is the area of the brain that controls emotions. In many children that suffer from damage to that area, you will see that this area is not fully developed or that the synopsis' are not firing as rapidly in this area as they should. This results in behavioral issues, outbursts of anger, and a lack of empathy.

The same thing is true in a child's brain that is under the age of 4 years because the prefrontal cortex does not begin maturing until after the child is 4 years of age.

On top of the prefrontal cortex not being fully developed, the stress can cause these tantrums to become more frequent and more disruptive. You have to realize that a child does not think logically as you do, and there are many things that happen in our everyday world that can scare them. You see, a child does not understand that the pipes of the toilet are too small to flush them down, they do not understand that they are not going to get sucked down the drain in the bathtub or that their uncle really has not taken their nose off of their face. They believe in a magical world, not a logical one.

With all of these confusing events going on around them, it is no wonder that they are constantly in a state of fight or flight. As adults, we know that when we enter the fight or flight state, our adrenaline rises, cortisol or the stress hormone is released, which can make it harder for us to think clearly.

Now imagine living in a world where you were unsure if you would be flushed down a toilet, if the vacuum would suck you up or if you would be washed down the drain in the bathtub. This would cause a lot of anxiety and stress in your life, which would make it hard for you to think clearly and cause you to have a few outbursts or unexplainable emotions. This is the world that toddlers live in.

What can we, as parents, do? The first thing that you need to know is that you should not react to a temper tantrum with anger. Getting angry is only going to add fuel to the fire, so to speak. You see, the child already does not understand why they feel the way that they do, they are already filled with anxiety because of the situation, and if you become angry with the child, they are just going to become more confused and have more anxiety making the tantrum much worse.

It is also important that you do not caudle the child while they are going through a tantrum. This will only teach the child that this type of behavior is acceptable and that by displaying this behavior, they will get lots of love and attention. You're only going to reinforce this behavior by showing the child pity at this point.

What you do need to do is to let the child know that you understand they are frustrated or upset. Tell the child that when they calm down, you will give them lots of hugs and that the two of you can talk about what happened.

Make sure that you follow through with this because it is important for you to understand why the child behaved this way. For example, if you are in the grocery store and the child is throwing a tantrum wanting candy, it is important for you to find out if the child was hungry then you will be prepared the next time you go to the store with a snack for your child.

There are, however, cases when this does not apply. For example, if the child is throwing a tantrum because you have requested them to put their coat on. The reason that this will not work in this situation is that for every second that the child is not complying with what you want to be done at this time, they will view it as the control they are taking over you. They are winning. This means that sitting a child in time out or just waiting until they put the coat on is not going to teach them what they need to learn.

What you would do in this situation is to tell the child they have a certain amount of time, for example, 10 seconds to put the coat on, and if they do not put the coat on, you are going to put it on them. If the child does not do as requested in the time you have given them, then it is time for you to follow through.

You will gently take the child's hands and force the child to put the coat on. This is not something that is supposed to be a fun experience or pleasant. This is something that the child should not enjoy and will not want to do in the future. The child is going to force you to do this a few times, just to see if you are going to follow through with what you said you will do. Then the child is going to learn that he or she is going to put their coat on when they are told do, whether they want to do it or not, and they will eventually do it on their own.

It is also important for you to know that the average tantrum does not last any longer than three minutes. While this can seem like the longest three minutes of your life, that really is all the time it takes for them to get over whatever upsets them and often you will find that they go back to being their happy selves, not worried about what took place just minutes before.

Because the child's prefrontal cortex is not fully developed, they, unlike most adults, do not dwell on what has happened in the past, they are not upset nor do they hold grudges. They are simply able to move on with their life and forget the feelings that they previously had.

This can be very confusing to adults because we find that half an hour after our child had a tantrum we are still upset about the event and may even find that we feel embarrassed because of their behavior. This is the time that we as parents just have to let it go. Enjoy the cuddles that you get from your toddler after the tantrum and begin preparing yourself for the next one because no matter what you do, it is going to happen.

Around six minutes after the beginning of the tantrum, the child is going to be completely back to themselves and will have forgotten that anything happened. However, it is important to know that if your child's tantrums are lasting for 10 minutes on a regular basis, you need to talk to your doctor because it could be a sign of something more serious going on.

What can you do as a parent?

Ignore the tantrum. If you are in a situation such as at home where you can simply ignore the tantrum, do so. If you are in the grocery store or some other public area, it is best to remove the toddler from the area, so others can enjoy their day while your child melts down. You see, this is not the time to try and teach the child anything. They are dealing with their own feelings and emotions, and you need to let them process this. After the tantrum, you can worry about teaching them a lesson.

Try to understand why the child had the tantrum in the first place. Is the child hungry? Tired? Overwhelmed?

Let the toddler have some space. We have all been there when we just need to get away from everyone, and that is often what toddlers also need. They need to be left alone to deal with their anger, to feel their feelings, and get the anger out. Let the toddler deal with his or her emotions.

Get the child sidetracked. When your child is in the beginning stages of a tantrum, one way to avoid it all together is to get the child to change what they are thinking about. Ask the child if he or she wants to play his or her favorite game, if they want a cookie, or if they want to cuddle on the couch with you. Simply divert their attention from what is upsetting them to something else.

Have the toddler show you what they want. Many toddlers do not have a huge vocabulary, often it is only 50 words or less, and they have a hard time stringing these words together, which means they cannot communicate what they want. Have the toddler show you what it is they want. Usually, this will end a tantrum before it can get out of control.

It is important to us as parents to remember that these little people who can bring so much frustration to our lives have only been alive a short period of time, and they do not understand what socially acceptable behavior is nor do they care. They only know what it is that they need, they only understand how they are feeling, and while it may be short sighted, it is how they are wired.

When your child has a tantrum, it is important to remain calm and remind yourself that there is a reason behind it. The child is not misbehaving just because they want to, they are not trying to be a bad kid, but the fact is they really do not have much control over what is going on. Let the child know that you still love them after a tantrum has ended and move on with your day because that is exactly what your toddler is going to do.

Chapter 3: Self-Esteem And The Middle Years

When your daughter hits six years old, she'll start to be more aware of the world around her. Home is still her place of comfort but she'll also start exploring new experiences and make new friends. Either she'll gain confidence or she's going to be swallowed by low self-esteem. At the end of the day, it's mainly up to you to guide her to the right direction and avoid the serious side effects of low self-esteem later in life.

The Middle Years

Major physical changes are still several years away but the middle years also have a lot going on for your kid. Your child will now relate with more people other than family. This means a greater desire to fit in and be part of a peer group which may play a huge impact on her self-esteem.

At around age six, she'll have some understanding of how rules work and may even create her own as the years pass. When she hits eight, she'll prefer team games and would want to win all the time. When she loses, she might not be able to take it well. She'll also start to show hints of being responsible taking care of her belongings more carefully. She'll love going to sleepovers and enjoy school if she has friends to be with. From time to time, she'll have problems with friends but this is pretty normal for most girls.

By age 8, she'll start understanding that other people have different views on things. She may or not have a correct understanding of right or wrong. Depending on her personality, she may act full of confidence or full doubts about herself. When she gets into trouble, she may also start telling lies or sometimes steal when she wants something.

Behaviors vary from kid to kid and at different ages but in general, girls at age six are usually demanding. At seven, they tend to worry a lot while age eight is a time for being carefree and outgoing. By the time she hits age nine, she'll be more responsible and independent or also rebellious depending on how things worked out for her.

Suitable Activities for Kids at this Stage

To help nurture self-esteem, it's important to encourage children age 6 to 9 to participate in activities and hobbies they will find enjoyable. The key is to provide the right opportunities for to them excel, try new things and hone their social skills.

To be in sync with what kids her age enjoy today, you can provide her a computer and let her enjoy a variety of games. Just be sure to set appropriate limitations on computer use. To encourage creativity, you can buy her art and craft supplies or building kits. You can also introduce her to music and dance or any other hobbies that she may show interest with.

Let her join clubs or sports teams. This is not only a great way to introduce a great hobby but its also one way to teach her about discipline. Sports, especially when she's good at it, can be an excellent self-esteem booster for any middle aged kid. While at it, you should also let her help in the kitchen from time to time.

What to Look Out For

While kids this age have minimal issues to deal with yet and most girls are usually well behaved, it is still vitally important for parents to pay attention. Even if your daughter has good friends and is doing great at school, she won't tell you when she does have problems. It is your job to know the nuances in her behaviors so you can help her sort things out when necessary.

Letting your daughter know that you are always there no matter what is one way of building her self-esteem. When she knows she is loved in both the good and bad times, she'll have better outlook in life when she steps into her teen years.

At this stage, it's also equally important to pay attention to possible behavioral problems that may worsen if not addressed early one. Among the things to look out for are problems with making friends, frequent lying, stealing or cheating as well as tendencies for bullying others or being bullied. When she's not doing so well in school, you might need to do something. If you also notice her saying negative things about her physical appearance, it's critical to be there to correct any body image issues.

Chapter 4: The Modern Kid

"Hey, drop that phone and come help me out in the kitchen." I am sure that this is a statement many twentieth-century women have had to say to their twenty-first-century kids. Growing up was never the same for us as it was for our parents, so why would it be the same for our kids?

The world is a large playground now with booby traps everywhere. When the current parents of this generation were growing up, child labor and large families were common. These were the things that shaped the children of the 20th century. Respect for your elderly ones was very paramount back then, and you dared not even dream of trying to do something that did not help your parents out with providing for the family. Children back then were taught to be ready for adult life at an early age. However, I do think it is still somewhat the same for the children of this generation, just a little bit different in methods. Now, children still grow up early. The only difference is that they are not just forced by their parents; they are forced by society, the internet and the world as a whole. There is so much knowledge floating around that it might actually be harder for a child to stick to learning something these days. Do not get me wrong, it is obviously better than the times when the only way a child could learn was on the laps of a grandparent or in a classroom from books that were limited in supply and got outdated quite easily. However, one problem the kids of this generation face is the difficulty of sticking to a single subject or course, just because of how much information is always floating around at any particular time. Now, rather than getting outdated information, instead they are bombarded with too many opinions, views, theories and so much more.

Another thing that is definitely different between the children of the past generation and this one is the way they worked. The children that were born in the 20th century were forced into manual labor, and little emphasis was put on school. Then, kids that were seven to ten years old were expected to start supporting the family and were placed in harsh working conditions that were definitely not fit for a child. A lot of children were born back then, and not all of them were expected to survive. You definitely would not want that for your kid, and there are laws in place now that would prevent child labor in most countries. There are very few harsh working situations that a child could be put into these days, but there are still things that your child can suffer from. There is bullying, which could come in any form. They could get bullied by their peers in school, it could be from the internet and it could even come from you, their parent. The problem here is that you have to realize that whether you like or not, your kid has been born into a generation with so many opportunities and they feel like they have an entitlement to so many things. It is your job to help them navigate this new world properly and make sure that they get the best training for the adversities to come.

Back in the day, the discipline was left to the dad and all the mum would do was scold the child verbally. It was what made this phrase so common, "Wait till your dad gets home!" Back in the day, the role of dads in the life of the children was to be the provider of shelter, food, and security. They rarely had anything to do with all the emotional aspect of the child. These days, it is different for the kids of this generation, as more fathers are taking an interest in the whole upbringing of their child. This is also possible because of all the technological advancements that have taken place in the workplace, which have made some jobs easier and more automated, thereby giving the dads more time to spend at home. Just like the impact of the mother in the life of a child cannot be ignored, so shouldn't the impact of the father in the lives of the kids. A lot more dads are now involved actively in the upbringing of their children, and this is a good shift in parenting for the 21**st** - century kids.

You might find it easier to blame the kids for everything, but have you taken the time to look at some things that have changed in the house, too? When you as a parent were growing up as a child, you definitely had more supervision from your mother and that was because she was usually at home. This, back then, was taken as a great privilege for a mother to be able to look after her children and the family. And of course, there is the positive shift in the current day and age for women being able to work more than they did in the past and get paid fairly for it. However, the society has somehow found a way to stigmatize stay at home mums. They look at them like people that don't have any ambition to live for. This has made it even more difficult for the children to get all the parenting that they need. I am not pushing the blame on any one of the parents in particular, but right from the days of men making fire by striking rocks, the mother has been the focus as the homemaker and that has not changed essentially in the current age. Of course, I already talked about the father taking more responsibility in parenting their child; therefore, the real problem here is the parent actually taking the time to supervise some of the things their children are doing and get more involved in their lives before they become teenagers and want nothing to do with their parents anymore. Trust me, they will get to that stage regardless; the real question is would you have prepared them for it, and would you have been in their lives long enough to be able to help them navigate this perilous and also beautiful stage of their lives?

Do you remember that back then, teachers were allowed to hit the kids and the parents were fine with it? (Well... at least for the most part). Then, in the mid-twentieth century, basically the mid-1900s, the children were spending a large percentage of their time in school, and the teachers were seen as the only guardian that the kids had to correct them. They were therefore allowed to hit the kids as they saw fit, and trust me, they saw it fit a lot. Fast forward some 70 years past that time, and it is now against the law to hit a child, and even though some people still think it is necessary to properly train a kid, I am not here to debate that. However, you would have to find a new way to discipline your kid, such that you can let your kid know that every action has a consequence and not all of them are pleasurable. One of the ways to do this is by placing a child on time out when he/she does something wrong. To go further, you can take away some privileges so the child learns to respect your authority as a parent. You don't always have to do something harsh when they make a mistake; some mistakes are mild and can be corrected by showing them what is wrong with their ways. Also, you can decide to teach a new skill to your child if they did something bad because they did not know better. Also, my favorite sometimes is to allow for the natural consequence of an event as long as it doesn't do any permanent damage to the kid, but nature has been one of the best teachers; so why stop her now?

Every generation has definitely had its struggles, and of course, so many things are easier today than they were even just ten years ago, so it might be unfair to start comparing life back then, some 40 years ago, to life now. One thing that has always been true is the fact that convenience doesn't always mean that life would be easier. Sometimes, we as human beings tend to want to do more just because we can do more.

One thing we definitely cannot ignore is technology. Are you kidding me, microwaved popcorn! I didn't even know that popcorn came out white until a very long time after I had gotten used to eating the brown ones we used to make in our kitchen. In terms of medicine, our children have a better chance at surviving childhood than we did back in the day. Also, they take all our worrying for granted because they didn't grow up in a generation where people died of the flu and children had a less than 50% chance of surviving childhood. The best thing to do these days is to make sure that your kid knows the right way to use technology. Because whether you like it or not, they will have to interact with technology one way or the other. If you try to restrict them from using, say, maybe a phone or the television, then one day they are able to watch TV in a friend's house. Then, you will have no control over what they watch and the whole purpose of restricting them would be defeated. The whole idea here is control! Yes, control.

You, as a parent, want to have control over the upbringing of your child, as hard as that might be in this generation. At the same time, you want to make sure they grow into young capable adults that are able to make important decisions on their own. The best way is to make sure you reasonably control most of the things you think they need supervision in, but make it seem like they are the ones calling the shots. For instance, you let your kids watch the TV, but you restrict the channels that can be watched with parental guidance. Also, in the end, nothing beats confrontation and instructional parenting. If you want your child to do something or not do something, then the best thing to do is to tell them exactly that. Kids these days have high emotional intelligence and they can easily tell if you don't have full authority over what they do; you would, therefore, have to show them that you do.

For instance, a kid today might complain at the fact that he/she is not allowed that much freedom, while her parents back then wish they at least had someone to look after what they did. Most parents now complain that their kids don't go out anymore, and they complain that they spend too much time staring at a screen indoors. However, one of the kids that was interviewed said that she gets to interact with so many people when she is on the internet, and she has been able to learn about different cultures around the world. Of course, too much of anything is not good and her parents make sure that she has some hours of physical sports every day, and on the weekends, she helps in the kitchen or in her father's garage (whoever calls dibs first).

All you need to communicate to your kid is for them to understand that you were born in different times and you are now in their generation, not yours.

Chapter 5: Aggression, Tantrums And Other Challenging Behaviors

Parenting brings some universal challenges that occur at all stages of children's development.

The challenges of parenthood can be grouped into three categories:

Challenges related to the child,

Challenges related to parenting,

Challenges related to the requirements and expectations of the environment.

It seems that all three categories are equally demanding, and parents spend a lot of energy on their daily activities to keep their family healthy and happy at the end of the day.

Many behavioral problems are part of growing up. It is very important that parents first try to understand the changes that each child has undergone during each phase of their development. It is necessary to determine which behaviors are desirable and which are unacceptable, always taking into account the age and degree of development of the child.

The advice and recommendations of experts, based on contemporary scientific research in the field of primary development, can help parents to overcome the problems of child behavior. However, each child is different and requires a specific approach.

There are, however, universal bad behaviors that children show, and these behaviors need to be corrected.

The child exhibits signs of aggression or often commits aggressive acts

Aggressive behavior of your child may seem like a serious problem. However, in most of these situations, children are only impulsively responsive because they are unaware of their actions. This is especially true for younger children - from birth until the 18th month of life when they still do not know how to express their feelings or emotions such as loneliness, helplessness, fear or confusion.

Nevertheless, in spite of the parents' concerns about the aggressive and irritable behavior of their children, it is a normal stage of development through which each child passes. Over time, growing up in an environment with clear boundaries between good and bad behavior and where rules and discipline are in place, their aggression begins to fade.

What should you do?

One of the best ways of treating aggression in children, especially from the first to the third year, is to bring the child from feeling anger and neglect to focusing on something positive, such as their favorite game, reading a book etc. In this way, the child will learn to channel his energy and use it for something productive and useful. In such situations, it is important that you address the child as calmly as possible, as this will help them calm down more quickly .

Toddler's tantrums

Temper tantrums in young children are usually sudden and unplanned and are often wrongly interpreted as a way of attracting attention. During the tantrum, the child often cries, screams, swings his arms and legs, and often falls on the floor hitting the floor with his head, arms, and legs.

Such episodes usually last from half a minute to two minutes with the strongest intensity at the very beginning. Outbursts are most common in children under four years old, but with some children, they happen as often as daily.

Scientists explain that it is a normal response to the obstacles that the child faces when acquiring independence or learning some skill. The child cannot find the way to express his frustration or anger in another way at that moment.

For most children these episodes of tantrums eventually stop. In time, all children will learn a healthy way of managing the strong emotional feelings that come when there is a lot of change. However, children who still have those episodes after reaching four years of age need some sort of help. If incidents continue during school, they usually point to deeper problems such as learning problems or problems in communicating with other children.

Stubbornness - How to teach a child to cooperate

Since their first year of life, children begin to insist on their independence. Your toddler is trying to do everything he or she can, without the help of adults. Due to lack of time, that often causes anxiety in adults and causes stubbornness in the children. Parents sometimes want to break the child's stubbornness, which again provokes their behavior. For this reason the recommendation for parents is to teach the child how to cooperate.

The process of learning cooperation can be difficult for the child, especially in the early stages of life. Therefore, it is best to allow children to see why cooperation is good and desirable by including them in different activities. In this way, children will begin to notice their importance and will be interested in cooperating.

For example, while assisting you in cleaning the house, your child will learn that teamwork can make the job faster and easier.

For a shy child, the most important thing is support

Every child is raised in a different way and faces different social situations, developing different mechanisms to interact with other children. Some children quickly adapt to the new environments and communicate easily with people whom they meet for the first time. Others are reluctant and will prefer to be in the company of people already familiar to them. However, none of these behaviors can be treated as "better" or "more natural" in relation to the other, since both are completely normal ways that children deal with new social situations.

While trying to find the perfect formula for caring for and educating their children, with the help and advice of experts, it is important that moms and dads also listen to their instincts since they know their little ones. In addition to providing a safe and stable environment in which they will be able to grow and develop, the best way to protect children from different problems is to help and support them in a positive way.

The solutions here are not always obvious and simple. That is why it is important that you always talk to your child. You have to give them support and build trust between them and you. That way, you will always be a part of their life even when their education ends.

Parents are naturally concerned about the safety of their child and want their baby to grow up to be a happy, strong, and responsible person. Sometimes, however, their good wishes are not fulfilled in the process. Parents complain that their child is not respectful. They often describe their child as being more interested in spending time with his friends. Also, parents feel like they are irrelevant to their children.

This means that parents have failed to build a close relationship with their children in the early ages. They need to focus all their patience on them and with a positive attitude, they can build a very strong relationship with their child that will last a lifetime.

Chapter 5: Parenting The Inner Child

The child that you once were is still there inside you. But you are no longer a child anymore — you're an adult now, and in order to heal your Inner Child, you must become your own parent. Even if the trauma in your childhood came from adults or situations other than your parents, the psychological wounds you sustained were not healed. The child that you did not get the love and support that it needed in order to grow in a natural and healthy way. In order to discover your Inner Child, you need to reach out to yourself the way a parent might reach out to a hurting child.

There are some practical tools that you can use to re-parent your Inner Child, but there are some emotional tools that you will need as well. The first is **Love**. Every time and every way that you approach your Inner Child must come from a place of love. Harshness, cruelty, and criticism won't work — these are the very things that your Inner Child is firmly insulated against. The traumatic dynamics that caused your Inner Child to retreat can be difficult to shed, especially at first. If you were parented by people who were critical, abusive, or neglectful, this is your primary model for what parenting is, and this parenting style will feel the most familiar to you, even if you recognize how harmful it is. For this reason, the second emotional tool you need is **Patience**. Healing doesn't happen overnight, and it doesn't always happen in the way that you want or expect. Be patient with yourself. Allow yourself to be vulnerable, both as a parent and child. Allow yourself to make mistakes, to progress slowly, to regress back into behaviors that you thought you had mastered. Trust that you are on the right path and respect your journey.

The final emotional tool you need is **Forgiveness**. Traumatic experiences are often humiliating, and our responses to them are rarely glamorous or heroic. You may have done things as a child that you are ashamed or embarrassed about. You may have done some things as an adult that were hurtful, cruel, or shameful. Trauma is necessarily external, and so there will be people in your past that inflicted the wounds you are now trying to heal. **Forgiving people who have hurt you does not mean validating, excusing, or justifying their behavior.** Forgiveness is about acceptance. In order to heal the wounds of the traumatic past, you must let go of anger, hatred, or resentment you are currently holding toward the people that hurt you. It doesn't mean that what was done to you was ok. It means that you are ready to reclaim control over your own happiness. By carrying anger and hatred inside you, you are allowing that person to hurt you and your Inner Child over and over again.

Re-parenting Tools and Strategies

In addition to your three emotional tools (Love, Patience, and Forgiveness) there are many different activities and exercises you can do to reach out to your Inner Child and open up opportunities for re-parenting. Everyone's mind and body work differently, and so not every activity will feel right for you. Inner Child Healing is a journey, one on which you will undergo some dramatic transformations. Who you are one day may be very different from the person you are the next. If an exercise or activity isn't working for you now, let it go. When you're ready, you can always go back to it.

Most of the re-parenting exercises in this book are spiritual, physical, and emotional. They are rooted in the arts, meditation, mindfulness, and fitness. One tool that I will not suggest here is medication. If you feel like medication is something that you need, absolutely speak with a psychiatrist or physician that you trust. Psychiatric medication is something you should never feel embarrassed or ashamed to take, but it rarely solves the problem by itself. If you want to take or are currently on medication, use your meds the way mechanics use jacks when they work on cars. The jack props up the car and holds it firmly in place so that the mechanic can safely see what's going on and do the necessary repair work. Psych meds are jacks for your emotions, propping them up and holding them in place so that you can safely do the work you need to without getting crushed.

Drawing

Drawing, and other forms of visual art, can be an amazingly powerful tool for Inner Child Healing. Drawing, painting, playing with clay – these are things that children do spontaneously, happily, and naturally. We only lose our artistic inclinations as adults when we are made to feel ashamed of something that we've created. Drawing is so ingrained in our natural human development that it comes well before writing. Art therapy is often used with children who refuse to speak or who feel they cannot verbalize their feelings. Inviting your Inner Child to color and draw can give you the freedom to finally say things you were never able to put into words. If you are artistically inclined as an adult, you know that the process of creating visual art breaks you out of rational, analytical mental states. If you suffered with very restrictive parents or an education that prioritized verbal logic, drawing can help you to reconnect with your natural, childlike creative impulses. Everyone is capable of making art. It's a natural, necessary part of our development. The stifling of creativity through shame or criticism leaves very real wounds on the Inner Child. Drawing through our self-doubts and self-criticisms allows us to speak with the Inner Child in its own language (Capacchione, 1991).

Writing

Language is an integral part of our experience as humans. Though we tend to associate writing with the intellect, language is deeply emotionally and culturally coded. Certain words and phrases can sometimes trigger deep emotional responses within us. Poets have known this for centuries. So have novelists, songwriters, and playwrights. Screenwriters in Hollywood know this. Bloggers, lawyers, and politicians know this. For this reason, journaling can be an extremely effective tool for re-parenting and reaching out to our wounded Inner Child. An effective strategy is to set up a two-way journal. One side is written from you, the parent, to your Inner Child. The other is written from you, the Child, to the re-parenting adult self. Writing these letters to yourself (or to other people in your life, if that feels right and natural for you to do) allows your Inner Child to finally speak in a safe, supportive space to an adult that it can trust.

Meditation

Stillness is an action, too, one that we often forget we can take. Did you daydream a lot as a child? Guided imagery meditation is daydreaming with a purpose, intentionally conjuring up a series of imagined images, conversations, landscapes, or scenes that ultimately help us to release feelings of anger and pain. After a heated argument, do you ever lay in bed imagining all the things you **should** have said? Before a date, do you imagine what it's going to be like in your head? Guided imagery meditations are like healing fantasies that give us the same kind of emotional release, but in a much more targeted and productive way. In meditation, you and your Inner Child can be together in the same space. You can hug, play, talk, laugh, and cry, all the things that parents do with their children to foster feelings of love, security, and harmony.

Chapter 7: Single Mom With A Baby - The Unique Challenge Of 0single Motherhood

Everyone knows that raising a child is not easy even with both parents around. Everyone knows that raising a child as a single mom is even tougher. Striking a balance between work and child care is the first major challenge single moms have to hurdle because it is simply impossible to accomplish without much sacrifice.

Single Mom with a baby is a major challenge.

If you are a single mom with a good paying job, chances are your work comes with inflexible hours and even requires doing some time after work - which means you will hardly have time to take care of your baby. Of course there are day-care and babysitting options you can consider but if you make use of any of these options, you will find yourself always rushing home to get to the baby before the time is up.

Besides, day care is going to cost you a fortune. The average cost of day care center for infants and toddlers range from $4,550 per year (**in Mississippi**) to $18,750 per year (**in Massachusetts**). Without savings and healthcare benefits you will surely be a lame duck. Even the low end range of the day care costs amounts to more than 10% of the average income of single moms. According to the Department of Health and Human Services parents should not be spending more than 10% of their income for day care alone - or they won't be able to save enough for the child's college education. (**You're lucky if the company you are working with is one of those which shoulders part of the day care expenses of their working single parent employees.**)

If you have day care, getting home after picking up the baby from the center is not the end of the day for you. It is only the beginning of your daily single mom ordeal so expect more single mommy tasks ahead.

You have to wash, feed, and play with the baby before preparing him for bed. After putting the baby to sleep, you will have to clean and sanitize the baby bottles, tidy the house, do the laundry, and oh, you have to eat too so you need to do some cooking – and don't forget you have to wash the dishes afterwards.

By the time you hit the sack, you will probably be too exhausted and may fall asleep almost immediately. Midway in your sleep, you may have to wake up to change the baby's diapers and give him a fresh bottle of milk. You also need to get up early because usually babies are up early. That means you have to force yourself out of bed no matter how lacking in sleep and how tired you were the day and the night before.

The next day won't be any different from yesterday. After feeding, cleaning, and dressing up the baby, you will have to prepare the baby's bag of goodies and fill it with enough diapers, wipes, extra clothes, and feeding bottles that will last for the day before bringing him to the day care center again for the new day. Afterwards, you have to prepare yourself for work. Forget about breakfast – you can grab some on your way to the office. While at work, you may have to call the center to check on how your baby is doing. Weekends are not going to be any different too because it will have to be with the baby all day and all night long.

You have to realize that single moms with babies to take care of are under a lot of pressure and stress. Single parent burn-out is not uncommon. If you happen to be a single mom, you have to realize that you need to be mentally, financially, and physically prepared to meet up to the many grueling challenges of single motherhood. There won't be any ifs or buts and there is no reasoning your way out of any of it. You have to meet the challenges squarely because your own child's future is what is at stake. Remember, momentary negligence can cost you your child's good future.

So, how do other single moms cope with this challenge?

Some moms quit their regular jobs altogether to spend more time with their babies. They look for other jobs with more flexible hours or settle for some stay-at-home jobs. This often means taking a huge pay cut which will also (unfortunately) mean having less money for health care. It is the only option if they want to spend more time with the baby or avoid paying for expensive day care expenses.

This is probably one of the reasons why the average income of single mom households in the country is comparatively low - hovering just a little bit above the poverty line. This is something that must be viewed with utmost concern by every single mom because if a child grows up in poverty or wanting in his basic needs, he is likely to have personality and behavioral problems in the future.

It is not time to throw in the towel though. If your current salary can't get your baby into day care what you can do is to establish your own support network. Sign up your parents, your aunts and uncles, your siblings, cousins, or any of your close friends and relatives whom you can call at a moment's notice to take care of the baby. Try your faith community members too. They may also be able to help you.

Explain your predicament and get their pledges to help you. Put all the names and numbers of all those who agreed to help in a notebook and place the notebook somewhere that is easily accessible. Make sure you separate those who pledged to help you on a regular basis and try to make a schedule for them. The rest will be your alternates – pitching in case the regulars will have some unexpected activities to attend to. The larger your support network is, the less worries you will have.

Knowing you have someone you can safely leave your baby with (**if the day care option is not feasible**) will give you peace of mind and allow you to take care of the baby without leaving your regular work. Just don't make a mistake of leaving the baby with someone you hardly know.

When the baby won't stop crying

Another one of the most taxing tasks single moms with babies have to face is how to stop the baby from crying. A baby crying non-stop can drive people nuts especially if they haven't had a wink of sleep and have to report for work early the next day.

The first thing you need to know about babies crying is they don't cry without a reason. They cry because they are upset with something. And, they won't stop unless the discomfort brought by whatever it is that upsets them is gone. The only problem is they can't speak to tell you exactly what's troubling them. You can only try to guess the reason why the baby is upset. Even the most experienced and the most knowledgeable parent have difficulty in finding out why babies cry - so this is going to be another tough one for the single moms

Here are some things you can try to help you find out why the baby is upset.

Check the baby's diaper. **A wet diaper irritates the baby's skin and makes him uncomfortable**. Change the diaper immediately. If the diaper is dry look for signs of diaper rash like redness or swelling around the diaper area. If the baby has diaper rash then stop using disposable diapers. Use cotton cloth diapers instead but make sure you coat the affected area with diaper rash ointment first before you put on the cotton diaper.

The baby may be hungry. Try stroking your baby's cheek slowly with hand. If he turns his head towards your hand, it means he is hungry. Another secret to find out if the baby is hungry is to touch gently the soft spot on top of your baby's head. It is called the anterior fontanel. If it is depressed, that means the baby is hungry. Don't worry, it won't do the baby any harm if you touch his soft spot gently with your fingers. The milk you are giving may no longer be enough. So consult your pediatrician – it may be time to give your baby some baby cereals

The baby may be having gas pains. They may have taken a lot of air while feeding or while crying. You can help him work the gas out by burping him. Another way is to lie him on his back, hold his legs, and move the legs gently in circular motions like he is pedaling a bicycle. Don't attempt to give him any other medication unless his doctor says so.

The baby just wants to be cuddled. Your baby may want to sense your presence, hear your voice or listen to your heartbeat. This is what he was used to while inside the womb. Swaddle him and hold him close to your chest. Try to simulate the environment he was in while inside the womb.

The baby may be over-stimulated. Babies get stimulated by everything around him like the noise, the lights, or being passed from one person to another. His immediate environment is part of his learning process. However, there are times when he may have had too much exposure and cries out loud to tell you he needs a break. Again, swaddle him and keep him close to your chest. This will give him warmth and a feeling of security.

The baby may be running a fever. Try touching the baby's forehead with your cheek. If his forehead is hotter than usual then get a thermometer and get an accurate reading of his temperature. If it is over 38O C, then he has a fever. It is a sign that he is coming down with something. Take the baby in a cooler room and take off any thick clothing. Allow the baby to cool down for a while. You can put a damp cloth on his forehead to help lower his temperature. If the fever last for more than one day, take him to the doctor immediately.

Summing it up, there are basically 3 things you need to check first to find out why the baby is crying – his diaper, an empty stomach, or a fever. If none of these is a problem then your guess is as good as mine. But don't despair because there are a lot of other things you can do to pacify the baby even if you have failed to identify the reason why he is upset.

Here are some ways to calm the baby and stop them from crying even if you don't why he is upset:

Give the baby a pacifier to suck. Sucking on to something calms down the baby and relaxes his stomach. It also steadies his heartbeat.

Swaddle and snuggle him. Babies are longing for the warmth and security of his mother's womb. So wrap the baby snuggly in a blanket and hold him close to your chest. This simulates the feeling of being in his mother's womb again.

Try to play some music or sing a lullaby and dance gently while holding the baby. This may be an old trick but it still works for babies today.

Hold him near a source of 'white noise' - like the sound of a washing machine or a vacuum cleaner. Their sounds mimic the constant buzzing sounds of body movements the baby used to hear when he was still in his mother's womb. This trick can be soothing to babies and it is worth giving it a try.

Bring the baby outside or simply open the door for some fresh air. Some babies stop crying as soon as you open the door or step outside the house.

Give the baby a gentle massage. Babies love to be touched. Giving him a soothing, slow, and gentle massage brings comfort to him.

Don't give up easily. The crying and the screaming is not going to last forever so don't lose your mind! Besides, as the baby grows older the crying and the screaming is going to subside.

Chapter 8: Truth About Teachers

Educators have to be so much more than educators in schools. Educators have become counselors, disciplinarians, psychologist, and caretakers; basically they have become parents away from home. It definitely takes a village to raise a child as the old saying goes, but you as the parent are the key to providing the support your kid needs to be successful in life.

Don't be a spectator in your kids' education, be a participant. If you have never been in education then you may not truly understand a teacher's reality. Before a teacher begins to teach your kid, there is this thing called a curriculum that they must receive, edit, learn or plan for the coming year. The introduction of Common Core Standards into many state curriculums has once again drastically changed curriculums for teachers. Curriculums are some of the most tedious projects to handle. The curriculum contains the plans for every single topic, lesson, and day for a teacher. This is great when it is fully developed but the process of getting there can be a major hassle. After the curriculum is intact then there is this repetitive and tedious process of creating prep work. This means preparing everything that will be needed for the students' for that day or week. This means spending hours on making thousands of copies, organizing, and gathering specific materials.

After hours and hours of prep work and learning the curriculum they can finally get to teach your child. Then as mentioned earlier the multiple job hat appears. Teachers are doing way more than teaching your child academically. Before a teacher can ever get to teach they have to get the class to an appropriate level of silence and focus. This can prove to be troublesome when there are kids who have not been taught to behave at school. Having to be disciplinarian takes up its fair share of energy and time. If the teacher cannot gain control of the class's behavior it will be very hard for the kids to learn. This is why teachers need your help to ensure that your child is helping to create a positive learning environment.

When a teacher finally gets a chance to teach they have to be focused on delivering the material properly so 20 plus students can understand it. Meanwhile, teachers are scanning the room to make sure students are paying attention and not misbehaving. When students fall behind academically, teachers feel that pain. They feel this because not only do they want the student to succeed but they question are they doing a good job with teaching.

Along with that they have to be an investigator to try to figure out what is going on with this student that they cannot seem to catch up or understand the material being taught.

As a parent you have to realize that, yes you love your child or children and want them to receive only the best, but you are not alone in this desire. Guess what, there are 20+ parents who want the exact same thing for their child in a classroom with one teacher. Just imagine the responsibility of trying to meet the request and needs of all of these kids and their parents. We are talking 20+ kids here!!!! You may have three or four kids but not 20 that you are responsible for every single day. Along with that, you have to deal with their parents as well who could be quite crazy at times. Some parents are great and helpful but presently it is not very common to get parents who are in communion with the teacher. So next time when you get mad about something at school and go off on some teacher or educator just remember exactly what responsibility teachers actually have to all of their students. If you have a concern take it through the proper channels. First talk with the teacher about the issue. If that issues persist schedule a meeting with them and a school administrator. Communicate your concerns and worries without yelling and demeaning someone at their place of work. I am sure you would hate to get yelled at or berated at your job, so don't do it to anyone else. Golden Rule...

Remember your job is 24/7, so when your child sees you going off on the teacher or educator then they are going to think it is ok if they do the same. Also, they will accept that behavior as a way to handle issues that they have in life. Hopefully, this is not what you want for your child; popping off and cursing when something does not go their way. Throwing fits is how toddlers get their way, not mature adults.

It is understandable to be frustrated at times, but you do not have to act a fool when you address the problem with the teacher or principal. Teachers are human as well. Teachers do and will make mistakes just like everyone else in the world. Pay attention to their track record so you can see if there are a few mistakes or if it is a trend, because then it may actually be a problem.

After teachers are finished working with you and your kid, they have to grade work. Teachers have to grade work while assessing the present day, and preparing for the next day simultaneously. I have not even mentioned the amount of time that teachers have to spend in school meetings which takes time away from grading, prep work, and accessing their day. Teachers arrive early and leave late EVERYDAY on a LOW salary. Now knowing that remember educators are human as well and they have this thing called a life outside of work. They have their own struggles, problems, issues, and relationships like you do. Not only do they have those things, they have less time than most people with 9-5 jobs to spend on their life outside of work while being underpaid. So, come on parents; you owe educators at least a well-behaved child at school. Educators are working to craft a successful future for your child.

P.S. If your child is not learning or there is always an issue with a multitude of students, you may want to have a conversation and observe what is going on inside the classroom. If the teaching atmosphere is not suitable then you probably need to transfer to a better school. Remember this, if the same issues persist at the new school then you may need to look at your child and yourself to find the real problem.

Stories: I recall a parent going off on my principal in public at the time because of something that happened in the classroom between the teacher and a student. Some type of physical altercation supposedly. This parent went on for at least 5 minutes yelling at my principal. After a thorough investigation of students and employees it was revealed that it was a total lie. When this parent was called and made aware of this information, did the parent apologize? Not at all. Please do not be like this parent because this is just another reason why the kid thought it was ok when making up such ludicrous lie. (Yes, your child may lie to you)

During the third report card period, there was a parent that came up asking for the second and the first report card because she had never received them. Then she wondered why her son was not doing well in school. As a parent you have to be highly vigilant and aware of what is going on academically with your child. You cannot just be a spectator in your child's education. You have to be involved and aware. Be vigilant of report cards, progress reports, and what comes homes. You may have to develop a system for asking or getting your child to give you what information that comes home.

Chapter 9: Guiding Children

The Benefits of Observing Your Child

If you have a child with learning and attention issues, and she's having a behavior problem, you may feel like there's plenty on your plate already. So if someone who works with your child—like a doctor or a school counselor—suggests that you observe her and take notes, it may feel like one task too many in your already busy day.

But you are the expert of your child. You know her best. Outside school, you interact with her more than anyone else. And you get to see her in many different settings, where there are many different demands on her.

That's why your child's doctor or school counselor may ask you to observe your child and take notes on what you see. He's not trying to get you to do his work for him. Your input can make a giant difference when it comes to helping him understand and improve your child's behavior.

Knowing your child

What You Gain by Observing Your Child

It may seem like your child's behaviour is random and her actions come out of nowhere. Or it may look like there's no reason that she struggles with certain tasks and not others. But observing your child closely over time may reveal patterns in her behaviour that can help explain what's going on.

Let's say your grade-schooler has a meltdown every morning, and you think it's because she hates what you made for breakfast. Then you watch her for a week, writing down what happens before, during and after her tantrums. Later, you review your notes. You may discover that what **really** sets her off is how dark her toast is. Once you adjust the toaster setting, she's happy to eat her breakfast without a fuss.

Not every problem can be solved so simply. But learning what to look for and what to write down lets you create a record that can help you spot patterns in your child's behaviour. Examining those patterns can often help you discover the source of a behaviour problem, even if your child herself doesn't realize what it is. And that can make it easier to find effective strategies to help.

When you take the time to watch your child's behaviour carefully:

You gather information about what happens before, during and after a meltdown or behavior problem. Examining that information can help you understand what your child is reacting to.

You gain insight into when and how to intervene to prevent a situation with your child from escalating.

You get a fuller understanding of your child's learning and attention issues.

You send your child the message, "I know this is tough for you. But together we can figure out how to make things easier, and we're going to."

What Professionals Gain From Your Observations

You're uniquely positioned to watch and understand your child. And your notes and observations can help your child's doctor and others better understand what your child is experiencing. They may even ask you to look for specific things.

For instance, a doctor or school counsellor may ask you to observe and take notes on far more than just whether your child gets upset when you take her out for ice cream. Does she try to read the menu, or does she just rattle off her favourite flavours until the server has one she wants? How does she interact with the wait staff? What happens just before she starts yelling?

Child consequences

Whether you want it or not, your parents plant mental and emotional seeds in you. These seeds grow as you do. In some families, they are seeds of love, respect and independence.

But not in all of them. In many others, they are seeds of fear, obligation, or guilt. There are many parents who act abusively towards their children, and such toxic behavior becomes consistent and dominant in a child's life.

All parents make mistakes in upbringing. That's normal, since there's no perfect parent.

But there is a clear line when too many mistakes, especially repeating abusive behavior towards children, lead to a toxic home environment that does severe emotional damage to an innocent young person.

Parents who carry a promise of love and care, while at the same time mistreat their child, are called toxic parents.

Almost all toxic parents say they love their children, and they usually also mean it. But love involves much more than just expressed feelings. Real love towards children is also a way of behaving.

What toxic parents call love rarely comes up as nourishing, comforting, encouraging, respectful, valued and accepting behavior? Toxic parents usually do extremely unloving things in the name of love.

That's how they cause great emotional damage to their children. Lost childhood, depression, anxiety, crippling feelings of guilt and shame, and low self-worth are only some of the frequent effects of toxic upbringing.

On top of that, we all tend to repeat familiar patterns of feelings, no matter how painful and self-defeating they may be. In other words, children of toxic parents try to re-enact their old, painful experiences in other adulthood relationships. Consequently, a double damage is being done.

Children of abusive parents tend to become their own abusers. And soon abusers of others.

One of the first best-selling books defining toxic parents and how to overcome their hurtful legacy and reclaim your life was written by Susan Forward.

The book Toxic Parents: Overcoming Their Hurtful Legacy and Reclaiming Your Life is absolutely an essential book to read if you had abusive, ignorant, inadequate, and alcoholic or addicted parents. It's also a great book to read if you have issues in your adult relationships, assuming your home environment was perfect (you might be living in a denial).

In toxic families, the rules are based on a bizarre and distorted perception of reality, putting children in a place where they can be easily abused.

Examples of such toxic beliefs are:

Children should respect their parents no matter what

There are only two ways to do things – my way and the wrong way

Children should be seen but not heard

It's wrong for children to be mad at their parents

And examples of unspoken toxic family rules can be:

Don't be more successful than your father

Don't be happier than your mother

Don't lead your own life

Don't ever stop needing me.

If children don't obey these rules and toxic beliefs, parents react by inflictive punishment or withdrawing their love.

Consequently, children blindly obey abusive family rules, simply because they don't want to be punished; and even more, children don't want to be traitors to one's family by not obeying, no matter how awful their position is.

As we said, children of toxic parents usually behave toxically to other people in their relationships – spouse, siblings, friends etc. Apologizing to all the people you have hurt, and all the mistakes you made (especially to your children if you have them) is an important part of breaking the cycle.

Genuine love creates feelings of warmth, pleasure, safety, inner peace and stability. These are also the loving behaviors you should spread among the people you love and the whole humanity.

But remember, becoming a true loving adult is not a linear process, but a road on which you go upwards, downwards, forwards, backwards, and inside out.

Chapter 10: Your Daughter's Development: The Science Of Growing Up

The adolescent period covers the years between eleven and nineteen, and is considered as an extremely critical moment in the development of the human body, not just externally. Although a person's brain continues to grow throughout his whole life, but even larger developments happen during the adolescence period.

At this point, you may suddenly realize that your daughter is getting, for lack of a better word, 'strange'. You may feel that you don't know her anymore. She may raise her voice for no apparent reason and she can be irrational as well. They both seek independence and their parent's love. Most of the brain's development occurs during a person's adolescent years; that is why it can be considered as one of the most important stages of life.

Just as any teenager may go through awkward growth spurts, they also learn new cognitive competencies and skills that come in stutters and leaps. It is important for parents to understand that regardless of the changes in her appearance (i.e. how different their daughter dresses up now or how tall she seems to get every day), the changes in her mental and emotional state can be just as jarring.

In the past, researchers thought that only infants have overabundant neuronal connections, which eventually get pruned into finer arrangements in the first three years of their lives. However, recent brain imaging studies such as the one taken back in 1999 by Nature Neuroscience, found out that there is a second sprouting of neurons that happen immediately before puberty, peaking at eleven years for girls.

The activities and hobbies that your daughter engages in shape her mental development. Her experiences and skills are also a factor. It is at this point that she either starts to increase her mental capacity, or go downhill from there. This organization of the brain is thought to continue on until your daughter reaches age twenty-five, with minor changes happening afterward.

With the increase in brain matter density, the brain's processing power is increased as well. Adolescents begin to form decision-making skills. However, their decisions can be greatly affected by their environment or what their emotions are at the time.

This is because the brain heavily relies on the person's limbic system rather than her prefrontal cortex, which is the more rational area. This is why a lot of teens do rash things like driving too fast. This can be extremely confusing for parents of teens.

During this period, young girls are in the middle of the acquisition of new skills, especially in abstract thought and social behavior. However, they are not always very good in using these to their benefit, and they even try to use their parents as experiment materials sometimes.

A lot of children at this age think of arguments and confrontations as a way to express themselves, but they may have trouble understanding what others are saying during a confrontation. Just like a toddler's tantrums, these outbursts of anger should not be seen as personal affronts. At their age they are dealing with heavy emotional loads and social pressure, as well as cognitive flux and they have not mastered any coping skills for these. Here they need their parents for support, those who have more stable brains to help them keep their cool, listen to what they say and become their role models.

Chapter 11: How To Raise Happy Teenagers

Raising teenagers is probably the toughest job in the world. However, failing to address certain issues that revolve around them can prove risky. This is because it is at this stage of life that children become obsessed with learning new things and trying out new experiences. If you do not manage how they respond to these changes, chances are high that they are going to succumb to peer pressure, which can cause severe consequences such as abuse of drugs and pre-mature sex that can lead to unplanned pregnancies. You can help prevent these by talking to your teenager about drugs and drug abuse, as well as the consequences of premature sex, and the importance of making the right choices. However, before we get there, why do teens really abuse drugs? Many factors can contribute to this, such as feeling of insecurity and the need for social acceptance. They care less about the consequences of their actions and usually feel indestructible, making them take dangerous risks like abusing drugs. Some of the risk factors of drug abuse in teenagers include: history of drug abuse in the family, behavioral or mental health condition like anxiety, or depression, low self esteem, feelings of social rejection, academic failure, peer pressure, inadequate nurturing by parents and a general belief that substance abuse is cool. Be aware that these factors might change with your teen over time.

Talking to your kid about drug abuse can be hard. The best way to start is to find the right time and a comfortable setting when you are not likely to be disrupted. Express your concerns with your teen if you are anxious. You can also share the responsibility with someone else in your teen's life.

Some tips for talking about drug abuse with your teen

Inquire about their views

Instead of giving out long and boring lectures, listen to their opinions and answer their questions about drug abuse. Watch out for their nonverbal responses to find out how they feel about the issue. Avoid as much as possible asking questions, but rather make comments to encourage them to talk.

Discuss the disadvantages of drug abuse

Do not use scare tactics. Focus on how substance abuse can affect important things in your teen's life such as driving, sports, appearance and health. Emphasize on the fact that even a teen can get addiction problems.

Review media messages

There are certain movies, television programs, songs and websites that glamorize drug abuse. Discus about some of the things your teen has heard or seen.

Talk about how to deal with peer pressure

Discuss about some of the ways to positively turn down drug offers from his or her friends.

Talk about your own drug abuse

I know as parents we may not want to show our kids that we have ever made bad choices in life but actually, what you don't understand is that sharing your experiences can help your teenager make the right decision. Be proactive as to how you are going to respond in case your teen questions you about your drug abuse. Explain if you chose not to use drugs, and why. On the other hand, if you did use them, what experience did you learn from it?

While it may be natural to assume that talking about drug abuse with your teen could plant ideas in their head, having these conversations lets them know what you think about the issue and understand what is expected of him or her.

Sex education, on the other hand, is equally a major issue among teenagers. While this may be taught in the health class, it is still of great importance to talk to your teen about sex. Sex education, as awkward as it may be, is your responsibility as a parent. By supplementing and reinforcing what they learn in school, you can prepare them for a lifelong healthy sexuality. Keep in mind that the subject of sex is always on the news, adverts and entertainment, and if you wait for the perfect moment to talk to your teen, you might miss the right opportunities. Rather, think of it as an ongoing conversation.

Some Tips For Talking About Sex With Your Teen

Seize the opportunity

When a music video or television program raises the issue about sex, use it as a platform for discussion. Keep in mind too that everyday moments such as picking up groceries and riding in the car are sometimes the best opportunities to have a conversation.

Honesty is the best policy

If you feel uncomfortable, just say it, but express the importance of keeping up with the conversation. If you find it hard to answer some of your teen's queries, offer to look them up or research together.

Be direct

State your feelings clearly about specific issues like intercourse and oral sex. Present the consequences constructively, including sexually transmitted diseases, emotional pain, and unplanned pregnancy.

Acknowledge their point of view

Don't make it a lecture or use scare tactics to express the downsides of sexual activity, but listen carefully. Come to terms with their pressures, concerns and challenges.

Go beyond the facts

In as much as accurate information about sex is important for your kid to know, you also need to discuss about attitudes, feelings and values. Evaluate questions of responsibility and ethics in the context of your religious or personal beliefs.

Encourage more discussion

Let them feel that it is okay to talk about sex with you whenever they have any concerns or questions.

Chapter 12: Spontaneity & A Baby? It Is Possible:

Once a baby is born, many people think that spontaneity must die away. This is not true when you take part in the joy of RVing. You will be able to provide the structure and security your baby needs within the RV, but the trip itself can be whatever kind of adventure you want. Perhaps you are the type of person who would prefer to plan out an entire trip; knowing where you will stop and how many miles you will drive in a day. This is a fun way to travel, but some people like the idea of 'winging it'. This is virtually impossible when you take a baby along. You always have to plan for proper places to stay overnight, clean restaurants, etc. With your RV, if you want, you can simply take off and drive and see where the road takes you.

No matter what your style is, traveling in an RV is a great way to keep yourself sane and even happy when traveling with your baby. The comforts of home within a recreational vehicle go a long way to keep you and your baby calm so that you can enjoy your vacation time to the fullest.

What to Bring Along

Probably the first thing you will ask yourself is what compact baby gear is necessary to bring in an RV. One of the first things you should take into consideration is where you are going to put the nursery. You do not need a big crib; you will need a small one and just try to find a suitable place in the RV to put it. You do not need everything you see in the catalogues to raise a baby.

For instance, changing table is one of those things. You can use the bed and you only have to use a changing pad. You can use the drawers or cabinets that you already have instead of a dresser. Another good thing is that babies sleep very well when they are in a vehicle, so you won`t need a mobile since your baby can enjoy the nature while you are traveling. Try to find a small baby swing, because it is essential to calm down your baby and it is definitely worth the space it occupies. If you are planning to go out with your baby, and trust me you will, then you will need a good stroller. You can place it in one of the storage compartments in your trailer. A stroller that has a removable covering will make the cleaning easier, so try to find one like that. It will be difficult to maintain it clean, just be careful with mildew.

For walks outdoor, a backpack is a good idea. You can put the diapers and the wet towels there; also you cannot go out without some snacks or toys for the baby. A small and easy to clean high chair is also an essential gear for the baby. If you find one like they provide in the restaurants, you can slid it under the table after you finish using it.

When you are shopping for gear, or when you have to decide what to take from home, think of items that can be used for more than just one thing. For example find a crib that later can be used as a playpen, or find a car seat that later can be used as a carrier and maybe a swing too.

It is all about simplicity when you are travelling with an RV, so a baby shouldn't change that much. When you have to choose which toys to bring with you, just think small. Why bring big trucks when you can find small race cars. Also try to find toys that offer choices, let`s say blocks or some toys that can be hooked together. Clean the box regularly, and always get rid of the toys that are broken, you do not have to pile up.

If your baby is over six months you can bathe him in a sink, but if it is younger then it is a bit difficult since babies at that age cannot sit unassisted. So, you might consider purchasing a proper baby tub. Find a small one which you can put it in the sink and also you can use it for washing the baby's clothes too.

If you are traveling with a baby , you will most certainly have to deal with laundry. If your toddler is active, then you will definitely have to soak his clothes anywhere and anytime. For this purpose you can use sports pocket bucket which is actually a portable sink.

If you want to feed your baby or put him or her to sleep you will always need warm milk. A portable bottle warmer will keep the liquids lukewarm all the time. You also have to keep the bottle sterilized, it doesn't matter what brand it is. There are microwaveable bags which will keep your things clean. During the night time it is also important to have just the right light. You can find a led nightlight that changes the colors and it will calm down the baby and make it easier for them to fall asleep in a new place.

Very important thing is childproofing the RV. Buy some safety latchets for rawer and cabinets. Use the highest cabinets for medicine and household cleaners. Protect the electrical outlets with small plugs. And you are ready for your new adventure.

Chapter 13: The Ill Mannered Teen

Teenagers today face lots of peer pressure to go against the flow and that includes being rude and crude. In fact, a teenager who is too well of a mannered teen is suspect in my opinion.

Often, the "over the top" manners you see exhibited from a particular teen is nothing more than manipulation on their part.

With that said, it is pleasant to hear teens be courteous to adults and even each other. Normally, by the time a youngster reaches their teen years they know basic manners that are expected in their social circle.

So, teaching manners to teens is usually not as much an issue as enforcing the use of manners.

If your teen is being rude to their family members then parental intervention is a must.

Whatever the rules of conduct are at your house needs to be clear, practiced and extended to everyone.

Your teen needs to understand that just because they are older than their siblings doesn't mean they can be disrespectful to them.

Parents are older than all their children but that doesn't mean they can talk to them like their dogs. That is considered abusive, and for a teen to have an unbridled tongue is the equivalent of abuse.

You may wish to explain it like this. There are big trucks and little trucks on highways throughout the nation; however, just because one truck is bigger than the other doesn't give him the right to run over the smaller one.

The law provides all trucks equal protection – regardless of size. As a matter of fact, the bigger the truck the more state and federal regulations that apply.

Teenagers who swear at their parents and siblings need to understand that such language is unacceptable and will not be tolerated.

Swearing at adults is not accepted on any level. When you go to the store, bank or ball game you are not allowed to swear at the merchants nor your fellow customers.

Swearing at anyone in public can get you tossed off the premises. This is simple and basic social etiquette. The consequences for teens swearing at family members needs to be consistently applied and severe enough that the teen finds the consequences quite insulting.

How To Redirect Rebellion

Rebelling against parental authority is as old as scripture. Remember the Old Testament story of the prodigal son?

Eventually the son saw the error of his ways and came home to a loving and forgiving father. Nonetheless, the son had to learn some pretty hard lessons in the process.

The prodigal son found himself having run out of his inheritance money. Consequently, the wine, women and song was gone as well.

The bewildered son had a reality check, and quickly decided to return home. Since he was reduced to eating and sleeping in the pig's pen he realized that even the servants at his father's house had a higher living standard than he did.

So, he returned to his father's house and asked for a servant's portion. Instead, he had a kind father who restored him back to the position of a beloved son and heir.

To help give a reality check to rebellious teens I make a very strong, and strange suggestion.

Although this may seem harsh at first, it can actually be fun for all involved. Pick a day that's convenient for the parents and call a disaster drill. Tell your teens ahead of time that on a day and at a time they least expect you're going to call a disaster drill that will last 24 hours.

There is more than one point to this drill. Nevertheless, it will serve to uproot your teens from their comfort zone and give them a taste of adventure, as well as enough discomfort to help them appreciate the fact that they have warm, comfortable beds to sleep in at night. There's nothing like a rude awakening to serve as a distraction, not to mention that it takes energy to be rebellious. Expend some of that energy on learning survival skills in the event of a real emergency and you will have turned a negative into a positive.

I'm sure you have enough imagination to structure the drill to both meet the need to prepare and rehearse for a real life disaster, as well as to accomplish the goal of helping your teen appreciate the strength of having a family to turn to in time of trouble. You can make the drill as elaborate as you wish, just make sure the children know it's a drill and that it will be over in 24 hours.

Doing things together as a family that are fun and adventurous often helps detour rebellion.

Teens love adventure.

Finding something they can be in charge of amid the adventure fulfills part of their need to be independent and a decision maker. If tweaking your teenager's role within the family structure doesn't relieve their need to rebel it may be that you need to seek professional counseling.

Sometimes kids will open up to strangers more quickly than to family members – especially if they know it is in confidence.

If your teen is disrupting to the family as a unit then it's very clear that outside intervention is necessary. My suggestion is that you seek help sooner rather than later.

Better to do something that is not needed than to not do something that was desperately needed. Although teens want to be independent they still desire the security of a family.

Therefore, rebellion that is turning disruptive is not normal teenage behavior and needs to be addressed from the outside in. Please do not ignore your teen's cry for help.

Many parents think they don't have the money for a professional counselor. Counselors come in all shapes and sizes.

Many churches have counselors on staff, schools have counselors, and there is usually someone in the extended family the teen likes and trusts.

We sent our teens to church camps that had built in counselors. Put on your thinking cap. I'm sure you'll come up with a creative idea of your own.

Furthermore, if money is the stopgap I suggest there is likely something (or several something's) that can be sold on eBay to raise the money for a counselor.

If your teen refuses to attend counseling sessions tell them you're going to sell their on eBay if they don't cooperate.

Sell them on the idea that talking out their issues is going to happen one way or the other.

Make a list of people you think can help them and let them pick the person they want to confide in. They may even add someone else to the list.

Check that person out and get the ball rolling. In other words, if your teenager needs outside help - that's a drastic situation that calls for drastic measures.

Chapter 14

Admit your mistakes. This is probably one of the most obvious ones, but communication is vital to parenting. Mistakes happen every single day. Everyone makes them, and it's a measure of the maturity of a man or woman with the way that we handle mistakes. People have struggled with this since the dawn of civilized life and will continue to do so.

There isn't a parent alive that hasn't felt the crushing weight of making a mistake. Not a single parent that hasn't felt the indecision that comes with not being prepared for a choice that has to be made. No one knows what to do all the time, every moment of every day.

From forgetting to brush your teeth to wrecking the car, mistakes come in many different degrees. They never feel pleasant and become easy to conceal and hide from the world. People naturally strive for the ideal and it's easy not to talk about the parts of it that aren't so ideal. It's even harder when it comes to mistakes made around children. They look up to parents as a role model, and role models start to lose their humanity, becoming perfect and an object of adoration, someone that feels the pressure to remain perfect. And it's easy to keep that kind of perfect air up. To maintain the kind of image that we want to appear to be in our children's eyes, the perfect super parent imagery.

I've found the solution is simple. Honesty. This works exceptionally well with older children, as the younger ones may not understand this as much due to the natural development curve of the brain, subtleties are often lost on small children that may not be as confusing for teenagers. A parent knows their child better than anyone else, only they can be the proper judge of what communication they're capable of understanding, but I've found a few basics to always be true.

Children watch how you handle mistakes that you make. If you admit that you made a mistake and work to make it right, they will learn to copy this behavior. If you apologize when you are wrong, they will learn that anyone can be wrong. That anyone can make mistakes and it's not the mistake that matters, but rather how you recover from the mistake.

As a parent, it's frighteningly easy to cling to our mistakes, try to hide them, deny them, stick to our guns even when we're wrong. I've done it many many times myself as I was walking through the learning process and none of us really ever have all the answers. There's no ultimate answer in this book or any other, but what's important is that we improve as people and as parents every day and that our children see us work on improving.

This can translate from the very small to the very large mistakes from spilling something then cleaning it up instead of leaving it to someone else to accidentally hurting someone's feelings. It's not easy to admit when I make a mistake either. When I screw up I have a desire to cling to my pride and fight even the concept that I could be wrong. It takes a conscious effort to swallow that pride and move to be something better than I was before. And like anything else, I'm still learning this lesson, but I believe that it's a lesson worth living. People make mistakes, no one is perfect and spotless. Admitting this to my children has caused a turnaround in their behavior. "I'm not perfect, but I love you, and I'm trying." It can be such a hard thing to say, but it means more than anything.

By admitting that you're constantly trying to be better you instill a lesson that they are worth fighting for. That they are worthy of someone who constantly tries to be better. It not only changes the dynamic in the family but the way they react to the outside world, adding positivity to their interactions and encouraging them to surround themselves with people that think that they're worth the effort too. I like to add a reminder that people that aren't willing to admit mistakes and try to learn from them shouldn't be the people that they surround themselves with.

In some families, this is harder than others. Many people aren't willing to even entertain the idea that they might be mistaken, and sometimes it's not possible to sever ties with these kinds of toxic influences. Every situation is so different, it's hard to give good general advice on it. This is a solution that can be very difficult to handle even in the best circumstances, but the best circumstances rarely happen, often because toxic influences don't allow for ideal situations.

I've found that it's sometimes easier to actually communicate about the non-ideal situation with the child, explain that not everyone understands that not everyone is perfect, that they often struggle with making mistakes like everyone else, but that they are worth the effort. And those that are willing to make the effort are the ones that they should pay more attention to because the people that can't accept mistakes are the ones that damage their own self-worth and the self-worth of others. This may not be something that sinks in right away, but it's worth repeating, over and over if necessary.

When it comes to people that want to spread negativity, I explain that there is no way to avoid all the negative people in the world, but it's possible to not let the negativity sink into them. They don't have to let the damaging people control them or their actions and they can be happy even if to many people try to stop it. The only person anyone can control is themselves and how they react to stimuli. They are only responsible for the way they react to situations.

No one ever holds any control for the way other's do things or the choices that they make. We can have an influence, but it's not worth dragging ourselves into that kind of pain for someone who isn't willing to become a better person. We have to make choices, and sometimes those choices will be made in a way your child can see. What kind of choices do you want them to remember you making? Ones that, while difficult, improve your life and mental health, or ones that bring you more pain because they're easier in the moment? Some people will never change, but that's not our fault. We can only control ourselves and our own personal growth.

There are always going to be problems in the world and problems in our lives. There is no such thing as perfect people or a perfect world. There are going to be people that don't like the way we do things, don't like the way we handle our problems. This isn't going to change. It hasn't changed in all of history and isn't going to change now. We are the only ones that can be responsible for ourselves. A child may struggle to understand this kind of thing, why the world doesn't always support the positivity that a parent may try to instill in a child, and we all have to develop techniques to prevent the world from taking our positivity.

Chapter 15: Smart Parenting Can Help In The Development Of The Child

When you have a kid with a sensory issue, you will need to be a lot careful about the way you present yourself before him or her. Getting to the point where everything is just about right is the key to ensuring that your kid does not lose out on a lot of experiences of the childhood. You might feel the brunt of having to go through that extra mile to get the perfect sweatpants for your kid who will wear nothing else; but, that should not de-motivate you or make you feel that your child is any less. Being smart while dealing with these kids will make sure that your kid gets most of the essential experience that is termed absolutely necessary in the daily world. This can be his recreational activities, schooling or as simple a task as eating. You will need to find creative ways to make it more appealing to them. Chances are that the same technique will not work twice, and then, there will arise a need to improvise or adopt a new strategy altogether. Do not lose hope, because that will only aggravate the issue. With care, focus, an organized plan and lots and lots of dedication, it is possible for you to decrease the impact of the condition on your child's daily tasks.

Delayed or slow developments to be dealt properly with

Not every kid responds in the same way. This is true for each one, even for the ones who do not have to face the sensory problems. Understanding how much is too much for your kid will help you receive better results. For this, you need to only encourage your kid to go beyond his limits and not force him. And when he does not reach the desired point, do not show your disapproval, and take it with the right spirit and work on your plan accordingly to achieve better results. It is easy and understandable that you frustrated with your kid's slow response to the treatments, but you need to also understand that some development is better than not having any at all. So you need to bring yourself to pick out what works best for your child.

What this necessarily means is that your son may not respond in the way that you might want him to when you try several moves and strategies to stop him from spinning around in circles. You might first try this by employing him in some other task that will keep him occupied. But you may notice that right after it he gets back to doing the same thing again. And this keeps happening for a long period of time, even after a number of attempts to keep him from it. In such cases, what you first need to do is, not lose your hope. Continue with the same strategy or move on to a different one, based on the development of the results from this one. On the first day, you could keep your child from spinning for an hour because you asked him to help you with watering the plants. The next day you could keep him away for longer at a different task. This clearly states the success of the strategy.

However, you might not really be happy with your child's progress, because you were looking for so much more. While expecting better results is not wrong, you should not dump your expectations on your son. This will only make him feel pressurized and in any situation, this is not going to work out for the best. Patience is a virtue that you will need to hold on to while working with your kid and that will alone reward you in the end. This can mean months of having him set at different tasks that will interest him more than spinning. Remember, your aim is to have him discontinue that behaviour; this can only be done gradually and not in a hurried manner.

Helping the child in getting organized

In some cases organization is the main problem that forms the hurdle to your kid's development. Tuning into the daily humdrum of the school and routine tasks might not be the most interesting thing for him to do. Most children with sensory issues find it difficult to tune out the extraneous noises that are inevitable while in the classroom. This may prevent them from maintaining auditory focus on what their teacher is saying, because, it is very likely that they are not able to differentiate between the two. As an extension to this, they will not be able to effectively answer the teacher's question. This will create an impression on the teachers that the child is disobedient or is not paying attention.

The noise in the cafeterias, gym class, hallways don't help either. They will only add to the discomfort of your kid, if he cannot deal with loud situations. If you are getting constant reports from the teachers complaining about how hard it is to have your son focus in class or respond properly, then it might be time to go and talk to them about the condition. Give them a detailed description of his situation and make them understand the helplessness on his part regarding the same. You could then ask them to make sure that your kid gets an environment that is more favourable for him to study in. This can be a position to sit inside class where he is away from most of the noises. Or a silent place where he can eat. You could also have him wear earplugs to ward out the unnecessary commotion that makes it difficult for him to stay comfortable. Most schools will be willing to help in such cases.

Your son may have the best knowledge of the states in the country or can name all the countries looking at their flag, but he has troubles listening to the teacher speak in class or sitting still at his desk for a prolonged period of time. This is not because he does not want to, but because his system does not allow him to. It is important that you make the teachers understand this, so that they can work around it.

Help your kid get organized and help him keep his things in and orderly fashion. You might have to do it for a few days until he gets the hang of it, but continue to teach him. If he is always losing out on the announcements made in school for the tests and other events, request the teacher to send a note with him, so that you will know and help him prepare. These are little things that could make your kid better organized with his school and work.

Proper nutrition and eating habits

Eating right is living right. Especially kids require the right amount of all the nutrients in their daily diets to grow properly and have a good build. Lack of any of these essential supplements will result in slackened growth and poor health. However, most of the food items rich in proteins, carbohydrates, lipids and minerals will not appeal to the kids. Hence, you will have to find a way to sneak them into their diet.

Especially the kids with sensory issues will tend to often have a specific food item, a fruit or a drink that they will love and take nothing else. Situations like these call in for disciplinary measures, wherein you will have to make them understand why it is essential to take green vegetables as a part of the diet. You will need to experiment with the different food items that your kid likes and prefers and then add on other essentials to it, so that you can provide all that your kid's body needs.

Make sure that you inculcate the habit of eating healthy and maintain a healthy variety in the diet. Avoid food items with too much sugar in it. This, while being very popular with the kids, do not necessarily add any value to their diet. Fizzy drinks, which are also high on sugar, should also be carefully avoided. Place in front of your kid a few healthy options that he can choose from. This will ensure that he does not stray away into eating things that will affect it health.

Subscribe to a nutrition expert. Since, this is a special case; you will need all the help you can gather. This means talking to someone who is experienced and has a thorough knowledge of the matter. If you cannot figure out what are the essentials in your kid's diet or if you need help in determining different ways in which you can have them consume green vegetables and leaves, then you could ask for help from these experts. However, remember that, your child will be only interested in eating that specific food item if it is presented to him in the right way. A nutritionist can help you by giving you information. But, at the end of the day, it all boils down to how you manage to have your kid consume it.

Adopting the right methods can prove very helpful here. This can be by including vegetables in the sandwiches or by preparing tasty delicacies that you know will appeal to the taste buds of your child. Keep away deep fried food from the diet. Instead of processed fruits, give him fresh fruits. This will add to the nutritional supplements of your kid.

Dealing with sleep and stress related issues

You will be aware of the importance of sleep in the daily routine. A good night's sleep will have people working at their bet potentials the next day. Disturbed sleep or lack of sleep will often leave people stressed out throughout the day. If, lack of sleep makes it hard for the adults to focus throughout the day, you can only imagine what it does to the children. Poor sleeping habits will make it difficult for the child to pay attention to the daily tasks and you will find them crankier as the day goes ahead.

Owing to the changing lifestyles, families have begun staying up longer and waking up earlier than before. The home culture has kids up to very late in the night and the school culture demands them to be present in the school really early in the morning. This schedule can fit in only so many hours of sleeping for your kid, which is often not enough and does not count as a good night's sleep. If then your kid cannot focus the whole day in class, you will know what might be the reason.

This problem is more prominent with kids with sensory issues. Not only will they already have trouble paying proper attention because of auditory distractions that sound more prominently to them; with lack of sleep they will have even more trouble now. This stresses them out and unable to deal with this, there is every possibility that your kid will throw a tantrum when it all gets way too unbearable for him.

You will need to ensure that this does not ruin his day in the school. Sleep deprivation everyday will result in stunted growth of the mind and the body. Without enough sleep, the brain will not have time to have some rest and will function ineffectively during the day, resulting in stress. What you could then do to deal with this whole phenomenon is to make it a habit within the family to go to bed early. Cut out that extra television time at the end of the day, because it does nobody any good; especially to your children. Ensure that everything in the room of your kid is properly set up and he will have no disturbances in the middle of the night that could result in a bad morning on the next day. Make sure he has used the bathroom and does not have to wake up in between to go to the bathroom, costing his sleep.

Adopting the right habits will help your child not just now, but well into the future to maintain a healthy lifestyle.

Handling the behavioural and disciplinary issues

You may find it hard to accustom your kid with trying sensory issues to the daily routine. It is possible that he does not understand the concept of time or the need to switch between different things at specific intervals of time. If he has to make a transition to a new place or a class while he was just getting accustomed to an old one, he will feel confused. So teach him at home from the initial days the importance of constantly changing tasks. You can do this by establishing a time schedule. Teach him to do a certain task for maybe ten minutes or half an hour, if it is required, and then tell him when to stop. If your kid does not understand time very well, give him access to a timer. This will ensure that he is trained to adapt to most of the transitions in the day to day routine.

Teach him the need to place a request for the things he needs. While you might understand why he won't go out without his shoes, you may not always be around to tend to him. For immediate needs when he is with people who have not much idea about his needs, he will have to ask for the things that he needs. Only then will your friend who is watching in for a while or your mother who has come down to visit will know what he actually requires. Make it clear to him that if he needs you to get his shoes then, he will have to ask you to do it.

When some negative behaviour comes out of him, although punishment is the first thing on your mind, do not be unnecessarily stern. Ensure that he understands why you are punishing him. Term the punishment as a consequence of his actions. Also, take care to encourage positive behaviour. When children need attention, they will resort to anything under the sun. This is often not positive. So, before your kid does something that is negative in its nature, recognize the right thing that he is doing and this will encourage him to keep at it.

Do not be frugal with your praises and appreciate the efforts of your child. If he managed to finish all of his food from the plate, then tell him that is a good boy. This will stay sharp in his brain and help him identify what is encouraged and what is not. Refrain from superfluous praises that will turn to no end.

Chapter 16: How To Build A Strong Relationship With Your Child

In today's frenzied world we might find that we do not have much time to spend with our children; how on earth do we expect to gain their love and respect if we do not have any semblance of a relationship with them? The purpose of this chapter is to reinforce the importance of maintaining a strong bond with your child so that they will come to love and respect and ultimately, listen to you. Let's take a look at the pointers to build that strong bond with our children!

Show a good deal of interest in their 'aspirations'.

Right from a very young age you will get feelers as to the kind of dreams your little children want to pursue; make sure you give them all the encouragement as you possibly can so that it will help them nurture the same. You want to take a good hard look at their interests and aspirations so they look up to you and respect you all the more, something that will come in handy when you wish them to listen to you, of course!

'Listen' to what your child is trying to tell you.

Often we are so caught up in the things that we are trying to tell our own children that we forget that they too have their own individual voices that need to be 'heard'. We have to ensure that we listen to them as intently as we possibly can and even validate what they are saying at the opportune time. This will give your child the feeling that you are indeed 'there' for them and will strengthen that relationship of yours with them like no other. Make sure you do not pass any judgments until you have heard them out completely – this will only ensure they will be a lot more skeptical about discussing things with you in the future. The very fact that your child is trying to tell you something means that he or she has a good deal of trust in you – one that needs to be nurtured and not broken.

Set realistic goals for your children.

Work with your child's strengths in setting goals that are realistic and can be achieved in an opportune framework of time. The last thing you want to do is burden them with tasks that are seemingly impossible, something that will only serve to frustrate them and not serve to cement the relationship between you and them. Instead it will be strengthened if you take the time to understand their strengths and work in accordance with the same to help them reach their potential. This will show your child that you are indeed taking a genuine interest in them and all that respect will only come flooding right back at you!

Allow your children to make those decisions.

When you allow your children some modicum of control over their lives, even if it is not all that much, you give them that much needed 'freedom' they deserve and you do not look like that 'control freak' all children wish their parents wouldn't be. Of course it might be only where little decisions are concerned and can expand to include bigger things as they grow up, but as early as possible you really do need to give your children some semblance of control over their lives in order to better that relationship of yours with them.

Eat together as a family.

You might find that you do not get to spend a lot of time with your children in case you have a tight work schedule, but you can most certainly try and ensure that you eat together as a family at the end of the day. You know what they say, 'A family that eats together, stays together', right? There is no better way to strengthen the bond with your child than to make sure that you eat together with him or her at the dining table. In this way you are ensured that you really do get a chance to meet them, after all, and it is the tiny snippets of invaluable information about their day and yours that makes for good healthy conversation that really works in strengthening your relationship.

Spend time on the weekend with them.

You might think to yourself that the weekend is a time that is best spent at home, in order to escape the stress that the working week brings. However, you really do need to carve out a little bit of time to take your child out in order to spend some time with them alone. So while your wife might be at home taking care of your two-year old, you might wish to take your ten year old out on that fishing trip you have been promising to take him on for the last several months; the one that you really didn't get down to doing after all. In this way you will be able to spend some intimate moments together with your child; those that will certainly go a long way in tightening that bond between you and them. It will show them that you care deeply enough about them to want to spend time with them consistently every weekend. And it doesn't have to be something as elaborate as a fishing trip; you will find that a mere walk in the park will work just as well!

Develop a good sense of humor.

You will find that if you are funny around your children, it will work wonders in relieving any tension that might have built up between you and them. Watch funny movies with them and laugh with them if you cannot think of anything funny to say yourself; you will see that this goes a long way in ensuring you come across as a person who is more like a friend to them.

Do something that they enjoy with them.

If your son likes to play baseball, make it a point to take time out to play with him every now and then. When you do the things that they love to do, you will find that relationship of yours with them has risen several notches higher. If you do not wish to play baseball, at least make it a point to be there and watch your child play with others!

Chapter 17: Common Discipline Mistakes Parents Make

Before you learn how to discipline your child appropriately, let's talk about some of the common mistakes parents tend to make. In this section, you'll learn some of the common thoughts or emotions parents go through when they discipline, and how these thoughts and emotions can interfere with discipline correctly.

"He/she's been under a lot of stress, and I feel sorry for him/her."

Parents often feel guilty when their toddler has to go through a tough time, such as being bullied in school or going through a divorce. It's natural for a parent to feel bad, because who wants to see their child hurt?

Allowing bad behavior to slide, though, is not the solution. In fact, a stressed out child needs discipline more than ever for them to feel secure. Show your child you can still keep them safe by sticking to the limits.

"He/she didn't mean to do that."

Children should not be disciplined for spilling a glass of milk by accident, but they should still take responsibility for their actions through helping to clean up the milk. Letting too much leeway happen because something was an accident prevents your toddler from accepting responsibility for the accident.

If you decide your toddler didn't mean to push the other child too hard and excuse this action, then your toddler will learn they can talk their way out things by using the, 'it was an accident,' excuse.

"I didn't spend enough time with him/her lately."

Letting your child misbehave because of your guilt doesn't do anyone any good. If you feel guilty, look for another way to resolve that guilt rather than absolving it by not using discipline. For example, do you need to set more time aside to spend with your toddler? Do you need to remind yourself it's good for your child to have healthy discipline?

"I was too hard on him/her yesterday."

If you offered a discipline that was too harsh earlier, it doesn't mean they get to do whatever they want now. It's essential you're consistent with discipline. Inconsistency will only confuse your toddler and lead to more behavioral issues in the future.

"Kids are just kids."

There's a thing such as normal misbehavior from toddlers, but it's important to distinguish this normal misbehavior from abnormal misbehavior. Letting your toddler get away with misbehavior by excusing it as normal kid stuff is detrimental if you're allowing your toddler to get away with too many violations of the rules.

"I don't want him/her to be upset."

Sometimes, it's tempting to allow your toddler to get away with something when they're having a good time and you know putting him or her in time-out is going to upset them. However, teaching them to deal with their negative emotions is one of the six life skills they have to be taught. You'll do your toddler a disservice by not helping them learn how to regulate their emotions.

"I'm too tired to handle this."

There are going to be days where you just feel too tired or weary to dish out one more undesirable consequence. However, it's imperative you get the energy to offer your toddler consistent discipline. Devote some extra time and energy to behavior issues now and avoid more issues down the road.

"He/she won't listen anyway."

Lacking confidence in parenting is a huge problem that prevents you from disciplining because you're afraid your child won't go to time out or they won't listen to you when a privilege is taken away. If a consequence is not effective, then examine the reason why your discipline isn't working. Avoiding it only makes the problem worse, and it's essential you gain parenting skills to discipline properly.

"He'll/she'll think I'm mean."

One of the largest parenting mistakes parents make is only to look at the short-term. In the short-term, your toddler could think you're mean for taking away their toy or putting them in time out. However, in the long-run, it's better for them and essential for them to learn. Sometimes, when your toddler is upset with you, it means you're doing your job as a parent.

"I always need to be the bad guy."

If your partner always allows your toddler to get away with behavioral issues, then it's likely you'll feel you're the bad guy when you discipline your toddler. Learn how to discipline together as a team, so your toddler doesn't view one person as the 'bad guy.' Establish some household rules and work together to enforce them.

You threaten to use time-out, and then don't follow through.

Here's why this doesn't work. Your toddler will realize you don't mean what you say, and they'll lose all respect for what you say to them. Idle threats will cause more problems than solving them. Your goal shouldn't be for your toddler to fear you, but it should be for them to respect you. Typically, a time-out threat is made with a louder tone because parents believe that if they yell, their children will hear them.

That's not true. They often just learn to tune you out.

If you threaten to use time-out with your toddler, do so with a firm, but emotionless, voice. Be prepared to follow through with the threat, no matter where you're located. There are plenty of places for you to find a time-out space for your toddler. It could be on the bench at the mall, or in the entranceway of the restaurant (off to one side, of course). Having to stop what you're doing might be inconvenient for you, but in the long-term, always following through makes time-outs more effective.

You lecture or yell while your child is in time-out.

Children need time to process while they're in time-out. No one can do that when they're being yelled at. You want them to understand what they did wrong and realize why they shouldn't do that in the future. Yelling makes them feel upset and angry about being in time-out, and it distracts them from the point of a time-out, which is to think about what they did.

Stay calm when you put them in a time-out. You shouldn't ever yell at your child because you model behavior to them that you wouldn't want them to model back. Stay calm and model this emotional balance for them. As a parent, there will be times when you want to scream, but it causes long-term damage that could undo the trust you've built with your child, so it's not worth it.

Your child is in time-out for too long or too short of a period of time.

Time-outs don't work for toddlers who are fidgety and under the age of two, and most experts will agree that attempting this type of discipline on anyone younger is just pointless. Time-outs are originally a way for your child to take a break, think about what they did wrong, and maybe feel a little remorse about it. Then they settle down and return to their normal activities. They don't make sense for children below the age of two.

Certain experts recommend time-outs be a length directly correlated to your child's age, so two minutes for a two-year-old, three for a three-year-old, and so on and so forth. However, some believe in equity for kids of any age. After the age of two, time-outs should be five minutes for everyone. Time-out shouldn't start until your child is quiet, too. Every child is going to be different, so an incredibly active-three-year-old might have trouble sitting in a time-out for five minutes, so feel free to modify the rules based on your child's situation. The important thing is to find something that works for them and be consistent.

You're emotional when you put your child in time-out.

If your child understands they're causing you pain when you put them in time-out, then they will prolong the pain and keep disrupting time-out so that it's punishment for you, too. They want power over you because they don't want you to have any power over them. Therefore, don't put your child in time-out when you're emotional or hysterical. Be quick, firm, and allow them to know you mean business. If they continually disrupt time-out, then don't berate them or act as if they're inconveniencing you. Just help them understand they're adding time to their time-out session.

Your toddler really wants a time-out.

You might be wondering why in the world your toddler would want a time-out, but some good examples might be while they're at the grocery store in a boring situation, or when they're doing something they don't like in the first place. Your toddler might jump at the opportunity to sit in a time-out rather than walk through the aisles of the grocery store one more time.

So how do you handle that situation? You don't do the time-out right then and there. Just make sure the time-out happens as soon as you get home, and let them know the reason as to why they're in a time-out briefly before it starts. Just make sure you follow through with the time-out!

You put your toddler in their room during a time-out.

Children's rooms are usually a fun place for them to go. They have all their toys, games, and entertainment areas there, which prevents them from reflecting on their bad behavior, which is the whole point of time-out. Therefore, time-out should be in a 'boring' area of the home. A chair facing the blank wall will work, but some people find this a little too harsh.

If you don't like the blank wall idea, then try having a designated room for a time-out. The laundry room is a good place. And if they're really bored, maybe they'll fold that extra load for you! Of course, you should always watch your child wherever they are and make sure the room is safe for them.

You don't give your toddler a lot of time-in.

The point of time-out is to withdraw positive reinforcement. If your toddler isn't accustomed to regular praise from you and doesn't have a strong bond with you, then nothing is being taken away from them during this time. Encourage positive behavior with your toddler. When your toddler does something you enjoy, let him or her know! This gives them a positive feeling when they behave appropriately, and wrong when they don't. This motivates your toddler to behave more positively.

You discipline your toddler with attitude.

Do you know a parent who tends to yell, become snippy, exaggerate, and just become mean to their kids when they want them to behave? Are you one of those parents? This behavior is not conducive to getting your toddler to behave positively. Rather than using consequences to discipline a toddler, you or someone you know is using attitude.

It's almost as if parents who discipline this way are trying to achieve emotional catharsis through raising their voice, displaying contempt, and losing their temper. However, research has shown that venting emotionally doesn't make you feel better, so it's no use to you or your child.

The first reason you shouldn't use attitude to discipline a child is that it teaches them that someone who doesn't get what they want should respond by losing their cool. Sure, when your toddler is misbehaving and throwing a fit, you might feel you have a perfectly good reason to lose your temper. They're being bad. However, to them, you're losing it because you're not getting them to act the way you would prefer. Therefore, when they don't get what they want, they'll behave the same way.

The second reason is it doesn't prepare them for life. If an eighteen-year-old is pulled over by a cop for doing twenty miles per hour over the speed limit, it's unlikely the officer is going to yell at your kid or berate them for the incident. They're going to treat your child with respect. They'll write a ticket, and then they'll tell your child to have a nice day.

That's how the real world works. When you step across a line, there are consequences, not an attitude. That's why a consequence such as losing a privilege is a lot healthier than a parent losing their temper.

You use shame to discipline your toddler.

When handling a toddler's missteps, it's imperative you not make it personal. Shame is what your child feels when you give them the impression **they're** bad because they did something bad. It's damaging for your toddler, and it has many consequences later on in life.

Research has shown that shaming a toddler results in a massive fear of failure as an adult. That type of fear of failure creates issues at work and in their personal relationships. Beyond that, it teaches your child to think in black and white terms. A person's value seems tied to their actions, so they can be confused about their personal worth and the worth of others.

You pay bail for your toddler.

Some parents make the mistake of cleaning up after their toddler's mistake. Rather than helping your toddler face the consequence of their behavior, they shoulder the consequence instead. It doesn't seem like it's a big deal when your toddler is just two, but it is.

Paying for the candy bar your toddler shoplifted without making them apologize to the cashier is an example. Replacing the toy they broke in the middle of their temper tantrum is another.

However, here's the issue. Over time, your toddler will expect you to bail them out for what they did wrong. Eventually, you might end up paying real bail. While it might be imperative for you, as a parent, to decide how much of the natural consequences of the behavior your toddler can handle at this age, allowing them to experience absolutely no consequences teaches them they can behave however they want.

So you've seen a lot of examples of how you shouldn't discipline your toddler, but what are the proper ways to discipline a child so young? Let's look at that in the following chapter.

Chapter 18: Single Dad: Rewards For Good Behavior Kids Will Love

Positive behavior is what every parent aims to develop in their children during their tender years so that they will become fully functioning adults who are well-adjusted to their environment. Among toddlers, positive behavior is a consequence of the positive influences around them such as the good behavior of their parents. Likewise, the negative behavior of children is the result of negative influences they have been exposed to in their environment.

The parent's primary role in so far as child rearing is concerned is to filter out the negative influences and motivate their children to focus on the positive influences to develop positive behavior. Positive behavior is what will help the children transition from one development stage to another until they reach adulthood. By tradition, parents encourage their kids to develop positive behavior by rewarding them every time they did something good or positive. Likewise, to discourage them from being swayed by negative influences parents punish their kids for every negative behavior they manifest. The system of reward and punishment is the traditional way of encouraging the positive development of children which parents have used for ages because it has been proven to be effective.

And in so far as rewards for good behavior is concerned, parents are convinced that children, motivated by rewards, are likely to repeat a good deed over and over again until it becomes part of their nature. In a way, we can say then that reward is a consequence of good behavior and is definitely a major factor that motivates and influences children to acquire and develop good behavior.

Children love to be rewarded. They love candies too. They also enjoy food a lot.

And so for a long time, parents have used food and candies as rewards for good behavior. Unfortunately, as people became more conscious of their health, they started to realize that giving food as reward for good behavior also encourages unhealthy eating habits and a dissipated lifestyle.

Parents today are now in the lookout for positive reinforcements other than food to recognize the good behavior of their children and to encourage them to continue doing the good deed. And this is not without a good reason. In the first place, today's children are already drowning with unhealthy food choices. They are already at risk of being overweight in the future which may even lead to more serious health problems in the future.

Giving food or sweet treats like candy as reward encourages children to eat even if they are not hungry - an unhealthy eating habit that they may carry over into the various stages of their development. Instead of encouraging our children to make the healthy food choices we are actually encouraging them to adopt unhealthy eating habits.

As parents, single dads must not only be concerned with their kids' behavior but must be concerned with their health as well. Kids love to be rewarded. Rewards are effective in reinforcing good behavior. However, rewards as positive reinforcements must not be at the expense of the kids' health.

A single dad can actually come up with tons of ideas that can make his child happy and encourage good behavior at the same time. All he needs to do is tap into his creative mind. The only limit to what positive reinforcements he can come up with is his imagination.

The best way to start is to ask your child what he wants or what will make him happy. In other words, let your child make the list himself and you'll be surprised at how simple and inexpensive are the things that can make him happy.

Some of these ideas may be as simple as the following:

Your kid will love it if

You can read his favorite book to him.

You take him to the library.

You listen to him read.

You bring him to the park.

You spend quality time with him alone.

You play catch ball or catch Frisbee with him.

You give him a high five or a thumbs up.

You tell him he did a good job.

You give him a hug.

You give him permission to stay up late and watch TV.

You give him a special plate or placemat during dinner.

You give him a coloring book.

You add to his collection of rocks, stamps, etc.

You give him attractive stickers.

You let him pick the story or movie for family time.

You give him stuff he likes such as modeling clay, stuffed toys, large crayons, Mylar balloons, marbles, trading cards, etc.

You let him plan a family outing.

You will never run out of creative ideas you can use as alternative rewards for good behavior - but never forget to add some words of praise or appreciation like 'That was a great job, I am proud of you'. You'll be surprised at how much more motivated he will be to do more good deeds.

To make your reward system more fun and enjoyable, you can give it a twist by creating a "**I've been good**" jar. Get a big, transparent jar and fill it with things that will make him happy – like small toys, art supplies – things he has listed. Seeing the jar filled with goodies that will make him happy is encouraging enough and will motivate him to do a good deed so he can be rewarded with his choice of goodies from it. Keep adding new stuff into the jar so his interest won't wane.

Chapter 19: Growing Like A Weed

It's amazing how quickly they grow. The saying is true: "Blink and they're grown." First you are bringing her home from the hospital and then you're walking her down the aisle. Treasure the moments.

During your baby's first year, her changes will be more dramatic than any other time of her life. Every day you will note changes. Before you know it, your little infant who used to just pee, poop, eat and cry will turn into a mini-human with a personality all her own. Let's take a look at the magnificent milestones.

Milestone Matters - First Three Months

The First Month

Imagine floating around in a serene setting without a care in the world. You aren't hungry or thirsty because your needs are automatically met immediately. Then, something happens. You are thrust into a world that is somewhat crazy and chaotic. You are forced to scream for your meals. Your cozy world has been turned upside down.

Now you get the idea of how your little one must feel. The first month of her life is spent trying to get used to her new surroundings and get in sync with the world around her. A newborn's brain is about a quarter of the size it will be as an adult, so it's not easy and may be the biggest milestone month ever.

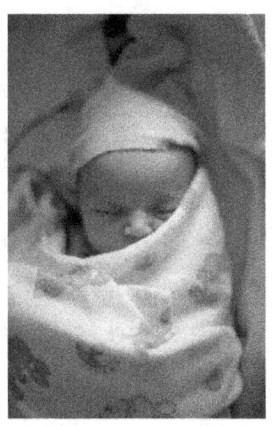

Babies are born with reflexes. A number of them are survival instincts that are programed into her brain. Some of them will disappear after time. Others will remain. One reflex is her grip and it's a tight one for such a pint-sized person. Another is the instinct for walking if she is held upright with her feet touching the ground.

Your baby will sleep up to twenty hours a day initially and then taper down to 15 to 16 hours in a 24 hour period where the sleep will come in bouts of two to three hours. It is never too early to begin to teach her the difference between day and night. Play with her during the day and rock her at night time. She won't understand now, but eventually she will.

If your baby gets startled, she will probably throw her arms and legs out. That's another natural reflex. Although her hearing isn't fully developed, she can hear and probably loves high pitches.

Babies are born nearsighted, which means they see things that are up close better than things that are far away. The first month she can see objects and people that are about eight to twelve inches from her. She sees black and white better than colors but of the colors, she sees the bright ones best. Don't worry that her eyes get crossed up when she is trying to focus them. Her eye control is not developed yet, but it will be in time. (If it isn't by the time she is four months, you may want to have her checked.)

Your baby will be able to sense taste more and more; the same goes for her sense of smell. She can tell Mommy and Daddy, too, just by your smell and also by listening to you.

The Second Month

By month two, your little bundle is catching onto things. She's much more alert and stays awake longer, too. It's exciting for the whole family.

Your baby can probably lift her head for at least a brief moment when she's on her tummy. She can also turn it to the side. When she is upright, however, she'll still need ample neck support as she'll be wobbly.

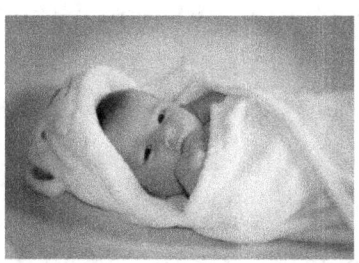

His arms will be jerky; he can almost get his hands to his mouth, but not quite. He will perfect that soon enough.

Your little one's brain is developing rapidly. He is like a little sponge, soaking up all he can like sights, sounds and sensations. You may notice that he is recognizing things, people and sounds. What an accomplishment!

Your baby is becoming more social, too. He turns his head to you when you speak to him and turns away when he is "all done" with paying attention to you. He is setting his personalized cues for being hungry, sleepy or ready to play. The more you attend to his needs in a timely fashion, the more trust he will develop.

Hold an object out and watch your little one reach towards it. He may even attempt to grasp it, tightly for a few seconds. His hand-eye coordination is booming. That is so fun to watch.

Be sure to give your baby some "tummy time." It's important so that he doesn't start to develop a flat spot on his head and so he can work different muscles.

The more you talk and communicate with your baby, the better. You can begin to read and sing to him, too.

Beware that on the second month's trip to the doctor, he'll get his first round of immunizations, if you are immunizing. He'll probably get fussy and may run a fever. It's best to cover the "what ifs" with his pediatrician before leaving the office.

The Third Month

The third month is a favorite for parents. With a little stimulation from you and Mommy, she will certainly shine this month.

She's probably getting her hands into her mouth by now, or coming really close to it. She is obsessed with trying, for sure.

Her senses are growing by leaps and bounds. She loves to touch things. You can help her along by letting her feel your beard or five o'clock shadow, your hairy arms and your nose or lips.

Her hearing and sight will be better, too. Brightly colored or sterling silver rattles in addition to toys will amaze her. She may even be interested in the baby gym now.

Your little one's motor skills are getting sharper. She will be concentrating more, too. If you pay close attention, you will note that she's beginning to "get" cause and effect, such as crying gets milk and smiles get smiles in return.

At baby's three month doctor visit, she will get her second round of vaccines if you are opting for vaccines. It will most likely be a mix of three separate immunizations.

Time for Big Changes - Middle Months of the First Year

Four to Six Months

Hold on to your heart. Your baby is going to steal it. You won't believe how stinking cute she'll be as if she wasn't cute enough already.

The little one who just peed, pooped, drank milk and cried is now on the move. She can't crawl yet but she is preparing to by getting her muscles strong. She rolls from her tummy and then from her tummy to her back—be careful and never leave her unattended.

She'll use her hands to support herself when she is in a sitting position and will stand with support. If you hold a toy, she will reach for it. She loves to play with her feet and will reach with both hands to do so. She can also transfer a toy from one of her hands to the other and will check out toys with both hands as well.

You may see that she is more easily calmed when you sing, talk or rock her. She is getting more used to noises and people around her. She loves to put her hands in her mouth (and anything else she can find, too).

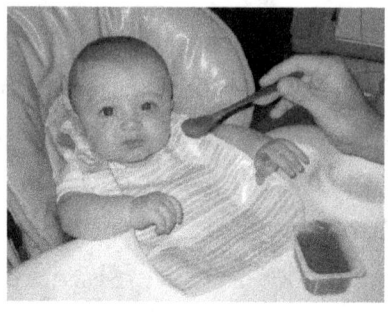

This is a fun time to start playing games with your little one. She will react when you speak to her or when she hears noises. She babbles non-stop and even does so to steal the spotlight if she doesn't feel she's getting enough attention. She loves sounds and the squeakier, the better.

Food is becoming of interest. She can begin to eat pureed foods and baby cereals. She anticipates food with an open mouth, just like a little bird.

Seven to Nine Months

Interaction is the name of the game at seven to nine months. Your baby is becoming more complex and it's exciting to see.

His body movements are more controlled and strong. He can sit without support and even moves from his tummy or his back into a sitting position. He is crawling or almost crawling. He turns his head to track people and objects and is beginning to pull himself up to stand. He imitates others and is a barrel of fun.

When handed a toy, he'll examine it with both of his hands. He may can even turn the pages of a chunky baby book. He is really checking out the differences in shapes, textures and sizes of things.

You will notice a much wider use of syllables and sounds and the combination thereof. He now responds when his name is called and communicates back and forth. He may obey a few rules, like "no." He is using his hands to gesture to communicate what he wants... or does not want.

When it comes to food, he can hold his own bottle now and can take his pacifier out and put it back into his mouth. He chews his food and can begin to explore thicker puree and even some mashed table foods. His tastes buds are maturing as well as his sense of smell.

Baby Steps Turn into Running

Ten Months to One Year

This age is when practice starts to make perfect. Your little all-star is ready for the game. He's getting stronger and wiser and is beginning to take on the look of a toddler. He is also becoming more independent.

One thing your little one will be mastering at this age is cruising or moving around while holding onto something like furniture. He will also take steps more than likely (and will a little help) may walk by himself.

He'll begin to talk too, saying words like "Mama" and "Dada." Yes, your heart will melt.

His grasping is being fine-tuned and he now can hold small objects in his fingers like finger foods. He will enjoy a larger variety of foods and is chewing much better.

When he wants something, he will point; when he wants someone, like you, he will hold out his arms. There's much less guesswork in what his desires are. He is communicating and you are in tune with his methods by now.

Pretend play is a big deal now. He mimics and knows he is adorable when doing so. He may show signs of being a little show-off.

Chapter 20: Be A Trend-Setter To Your Step Children

There are components of child rearing that step parents can neglect, maybe in light of the fact that they feel that they do not have any significant bearing to them, and one of these is being a role model. Indeed, viewing yourself as a trend-setter can be exceptionally useful in making the right attitude for a wide range of issues that come up in ordinary family life. A trend-setter leads by example rather than by brutal control. A trend-setter fortifies positive practices inside the family. A trend-setter approaches others with deference.

There are four keys things step parents can do to enhance family relationships by leading by example:

Activities talk loudest: Youngsters specifically react much better to activities than words. Whatever you say to them, it frequently feels like your remarks are failing to attract anyone's attention. Then again, the way you manage strife in the family home is liable to be reflected by your youngsters when they manage their own particular emergencies in later life. This is a calming thought. As grown-ups we have years of experience to draw upon when we confront challenging or enthusiastic circumstances. We may not generally hit the nail on the head but rather by halting, thinking and considering the effect our conduct will have on our stepchildren, we will probably settle on the right choices and act in the most ideal way.

Parent v friend: Attempting to be your kid or stepchild's closest companion as opposed to their instructor is a trap numerous parents and step parents fall into. It is especially hard for step parents who successfully need to wind up unplanned parents regardless of the fact that they have no earlier learning or experience of raising a family. As an outcast it can feel less demanding to be a companion than a conventional parent and this is something to be careful about.

Being a parent is challenging and it sometimes feel like you are in charge of everything your step child says, thinks or does. It is more essential for them to have somebody who can help them work out systems for adapting to their sentiments and the obstacles that life puts in their way than it is for them to have an additional companion in the house.

Have a ton of fun: Child rearing can be extreme, yet it can be fun as well. It benefits everybody to relax occasionally and have a ton of fun, especially as a family. The most intense way youngsters learn is by observing how the grown-ups around them carry on.

Setting them up for adulthood: A parent's role is to support kids to end up youthful grown-ups and youthful grown-ups into adults. As step children get to be adolescents and young people get to be grown-ups, the role of the parent changes and it is never too soon to get ready for this. By getting to know each other as a step family you can assemble connections that will make every stage less demanding and help you bolster each other through life's voyage. It is likewise vital to invest balanced energy with every individual from the family so you can become more acquainted with each other well in a casual situation without rivalry from different identities inside the house. Securities are not produced overnight and tolerance is fundamental, but after a time the interest in communication and relationship building will harvest rich prizes.

As a parent, whether biological or step parent, you are a trend-setter. The state of affairs that have prompted your step family condition are close to home and the feelings might be crude, however, the way you manage that together is the thing that will shape your future and that of the kids in your step family. So recall that every time you manage an issue, however enormous or little, your step children will watch and learn. Ensure they learn sound lessons and grow up feeling certain and adored.

Chapter 21: What Do I Do If I Find My Teenager Is Using Technology In An Inappropriate Way?

This is one of those questions that would have never been in a parenting book from 20 years ago, but it's very important in today's day in age. With the accessibility to pornography, the privacy of mobile devices, and the fact that most teenagers have at least one of their own electronic devices to use, this is becoming a major concern for many parents.

The first thing that you need to do is sit down with your teenager and let them know that you love them no matter what. We've mentioned that in all of the above explanations, and it still applies here. This is probably going to be one of the most sensitive topics that you will ever approach with your teenager with, and they will likely need to hear that as the conversation goes on.

You need to go into the conversation and realize that, yes, your teenager is going to get upset and/or defensive. Why? Because you likely had to invade their privacy a bit in order to find out. So, as you would expect, they would get defensive and maybe even angry that you found out about their browsing habits. They may yell at you and even storm up to their room in protest. Let them cool off a bit before talking to them more.

When you talk to them, you want to approach them with the sense that you are concerned about them. Fine, they did something wrong (and they do deserve some sort of retribution, whether it be taking away their privileges on electronic devices or something similar), but the more important part is how detrimental those things can be for them. If they're sharing nude pictures with a boyfriend or girlfriend, which can be posted online if something goes awry. Pornography has been shown to cause a number of mental and relational issues. Let them know that you're more concerned about them then the fact that they were looking at nude pictures. They may not be happy with you, but you have to stand your ground. You also have to share healthy alternatives that you both agree on. Even though they may be angry with you at first, they're going to realize that you were right and they will appreciate you for standing your ground.

Chapter 22: Lesson On Parental Authority

The dynamics of most of the parent-child relationships today is very different from how things generally were in the past. Although not absolutely true, it's safe to say that decades ago the role of parents and children was clearly defined: parents provide for and discipline their kids, while the children went to school and followed what was told them by their elders. Today, however, the parent-child relationship has become more complex. A lot of people have now become more lenient in their parenting style. There is actually nothing wrong with this as long as you make sure that you are still primarily a parent to your children, and not just a friend or worse, a confidante.

Why You Should Not Be a "Friend" to Your Kids

First and foremost, a disclaimer: the title of this particular subsection does not imply that there is no room for friendship between parents and their children. It just means that you should refrain from being a friend first and then a parent, second, to your kids. You are not doing them any favors by encouraging them to see you as a "friend" or a confidante. If you don't assume your functional role as a parent and set limits with your children, they will likely grow up with issues, in particular when it comes to recognizing and respecting authority. Also, if you neglect to place importance in your function as a parent, you won't be helping in your kids' holistic development.

This is not to say, though, that you should totally distance yourself from your children. As said earlier, it is okay for you to be friends with them, but make sure that what you have with your kids is responsible friendship.

Asserting Parental Authority

As your children get older, there will be instances when you will feel like you are being disrespected or your authority is being questioned. These are a normal part of growing up: kids rebel against their parents to see how far they can push the boundaries or limits you've set. However, make sure that you take pains to assert your parental authority when you think they are crossing the line; otherwise, they'll assume that what they're doing is ok and you'll have a harder time disciplining them. Here's a short guide on how to assert your authority as a parent when your kids are acting out:

Have a plan and talk to your children about it. The first step to asserting your authority as a parent is to create a game plan. The best way to do this is to come up with a list of what you will do when your kids act out. This may seem a bit odd, but having a list will help you be consistent with your reaction towards a specific negative behavior, which is very important. Once you have a plan, talk to your children about it so that they know about the changes that will be happening. Make sure that you tell them about the consequences for bad behavior, as this information will discourage them from acting out time and time again.

Talk to your kids after they act out. When your kids do act out, speak with them about the incident. It is important in this step that you ask what they want to accomplish with their behavior, as well as what they would do differently the next time they're in a similar situation. This will encourage them to think of other ways for coping with the negative feelings that may arise if things don't go their way.

Brush off your worries about "assumed judgment". A lot of parents lose their authority because they are afraid of what other people will say if they discipline their children in public, which is what "assumed judgment" is. If you want your kids to recognize your authority, don't worry so much about image; instead, call them out on their behavior and mete out the consequences appropriate to their behavior which you talked to them about.

Be firm with your parenting. Don't back down and/or give in to the demands of your kids who are acting out. Even if they tell you that they hate you (an expression that has resulted in many parents failing in their efforts to assert authority), stand your ground. Otherwise, they'll use the "I hate you" phrase on you every time so that they'll get their way.

Seek outside assistance. Asserting parental authority is not in any way easy, so it's but right that you take all the help you can get. Try reading the works of or talking to experts about the matter. You can also join groups of parents with similar objectives so that you have a support system: this will make it easier for you to accomplish your goal.

Conclusion

Thank you again for downloading this book!

I hope this book was able to help you to gain a better approach and understanding of the parenting world.

The next step is to start implementing and making use of the knowledge you have acquired from this book, and to recommend it to those who you believe are interested alongside you!

Thank you and good luck!

www.ingramcontent.com/pod-product-compliance
Lightning Source LLC
Chambersburg PA
CBHW072012070526
44583CB00015B/1451